P R E S E N T E D   T O :

_ _ _ _ _ _ _ _ _ _ _ _ _ _ _ _ _ _ _ _

F R O M :

_ _ _ _ _ _ _ _ _ _ _ _ _ _ _ _ _ _ _ _

D A T E :

_ _ _ _ _ _ _ _ _ _ _ _ _ _ _ _ _ _ _ _

God's Little Devotional Book for Boys

God's Little Devotional Book for Boys

HONOR HB BOOKS

FROM DAVID C. COOK

GOD'S LITTLE DEVOTIONAL BOOK FOR BOYS
Published by Honor Books®, an imprint of
David C. Cook
4050 Lee Vance View
Colorado Springs, CO 80918 U.S.A.

David C. Cook Distribution Canada
55 Woodslee Avenue, Paris, Ontario, Canada N3L 3E5

David C. Cook U.K., Kingsway Communications
Eastbourne, East Sussex BN23 6NT, England

David C. Cook and the graphic circle C logo
are registered trademarks of Cook Communications Ministries.

ISBN 978-1-56292-201-6

© 2004 by Bordon Books

Developed by Bordon Books
6532 E. 71st St. Suite 105
Tulsa, OK 74133

Printed in the United States of America
First Edition 2004

5 6 7 8 9 10 11 12
012808

INTRODUCTION

How do you grow a man of God? Start when he is a boy and train him up to it. His parents and those who love him fill him with God's love and goodness, starting when he is your age or younger. This wonderful devotional book is filled with fun stories, powerful scriptures, and guiding life principles written to help a young man, just like you, become all that God wants him to be.

You will experience God's presence and guidance through the stories about boys your own age. You can learn life-changing, spiritual principles on faith, friendship, kindness, and many other Christian values. Find out how much God loves you, that in His eyes you are great, and that strength and godliness go together.

With *God's Little Devotional Book for Boys*, you can take a quiet break from school and extracurricular activities to discover the God who loves you, knows you, and wants you to become all that you were created by Him to be.

In Search of a Friend

A friend is one who knows us but loves us anyway.

———— ■ ————

Tanner trudged down the driveway to the bus stop. It was only the third day of school, and already he hated it. He looked up to see the bus turning the corner into his street. The bus door creaked closed behind him. Tanner was thankful to find an empty seat close to the front. Quentin, his best friend since first grade, usually saved a seat for him but had moved away weeks before school began.

Tanner smiled as he remembered the time last year when he snuck two frogs onto the bus. Quentin had taken a peek into the can and dropped it. Girls screamed and stood on their seats while Tanner and Quentin crawled around trying to recapture them.

"Hey, can I sit here?"

"Yeah, sure ..." Tanner said. Lost in his frog memory, Tanner hadn't noticed that the bus had filled up. They were almost to school.

"My name's Ben." The stocky boy stuck out his hand.

Tanner accepted Ben's firm handshake and said, "I'm

Tanner. You new here?"

"Yeah," Ben said.

The bus stopped. Ben stood up and said, "I thought it would be hard to make friends at a new school, but introducing myself works great. I've met a bunch of guys. You can eat lunch with us if you want."

Wow! I prayed for God to give me a friend since Quentin moved away. Ben seems like a nice guy, Tanner thought. "Yeah, see you at lunch," he said to Ben as they stepped off the bus.

Ben nodded yes.

As Tanner headed down the hall, he called to boys he had met last spring during baseball season, "Hi, Jake! Hi, Matt." They waved back. *Yeah! I can be friendly too.* "God, You can help me make lots of friends," Tanner prayed.

A man *who has* friends must himself be friendly.
Proverbs 18:24 NKJV

WANT FRIENDS? BE FRIENDLY.

When was the last time you made a new friend? People who make friends smile, look you in the eyes, and learn your name. Pray and ask God to help you be a friend.

Not Just Me

The least used words by an unselfish person
are I, me, my, and mine.

———— ◆ ————

Ryan was bummed. *How could anyone think a family portrait was more important than the championship baseball game?* he reasoned. He pitched his baseball uniform into the bottom of his closet and buttoned his dress shirt.

His mother had been adamant: "We are going to do this." Even his dad was on her side this time. The whole family—aunts, uncles, cousins—all sixteen of them were going to be photographed.

"Dad, that'll take forever!" Ryan had grumbled last night. Today he hadn't said anything, but moped around the house getting ready.

"Ryan, are you ready?" Dad called as he walked into Ryan's bedroom.

"Yeah!"

Dad motioned for Ryan to take a seat on the bed. "Ryan, I know your baseball game is really important to you, but there will be many more ball games. Remember how sad we all were when Pawpaw died two years ago?"

Ryan shook his head yes, as he felt a lump rise up in his

throat. He didn't like to think about how much he missed him.

"Mom wishes she'd taken time for a family photo when he was still with us. We want to do that with Grandpa and Grandma now while we still can. Can you please help Mom and me remember this time as special?"

Ryan nodded his head again. Now he understood. Photographs of Pawpaw were so special to his mom now. She put the few pictures she had of him around the house to help her remember special times.

Ryan bowed his head as soon as his dad left the room. "God, I'm sorry I was selfish and only thinking of my baseball game and what I wanted to do. Forgive me, and help me make this time a fun time to remember for all of our family—my cousin, Timmy, who is usually a pain, included. Amen."

As God's chosen people, holy and dearly loved,
clothe yourselves with compassion, kindness, humility,
gentleness and patience.
Colossians 3:12 NIV

CONSIDER OTHERS.

Do you think everything should be about you and what you want to do? Of course not. But sometimes it is hard to remember, isn't it? Ask God to help you remember the feelings of others.

Words for the Critic

Keep away from people who try to belittle your ambition. Small people always do that, but the really great [people] make you feel that you, too, can become great.

———— ■ ————

"I've about had it with Kyle," David steamed. He set down the glass in his hand with such a thud that he thought it might break.

"What happened?" David's mom asked.

"No matter what I say, Kyle spouts off, 'Why'd you say that? That was lame.' If I get a base hit, Kyle says, 'Too bad you didn't hit a home run.' If I have an idea, Kyle says, 'That's dumb.' He never comes up with a good idea, but he shoots down everything I say or do."

"Sounds as if you have a personal critic," Mom said.

"Well, I don't need one. I may not always be the best, but I don't need Kyle slamming me all the time—especially when he doesn't do any better. In fact, he usually does worse."

"Critics can be like that," Mom said. "They sometimes put down other people to try to make themselves look better."

"But what do I say to Kyle? I feel like calling him a jerk and then never speaking to him again."

"Try giving him a compliment. Find something good to say about him."

"Like what?"

"Oh, like, 'Hey, I hear you got a good grade on your spelling test' or 'I like your new shirt.' If he gives you a bad review, give him a good one. Ask God to show you something good you can say and really mean it. My guess is that you might see a turn-around in Kyle."

David tried his mom's idea. The first few times Kyle just stared back at David's response, but then he stopped his cutting remarks completely. *And the funny thing,* David thought, *was that Kyle didn't even know why his criticism suddenly became a bad idea!*

Remember

A gentle answer turns away wrath,
But a harsh word stirs up anger.
Proverbs 15:1 NASB

SPEAK WHAT YOU WANT TO HEAR.

You Can Do It!

How we respond is always much more important than anything others say to us or about us. Ask God today, "Please help me to speak positive words to others when I hear negative words from them."

Taking the Lead

I don't know the key to success, but the key to failure is trying to please everybody.

Neil stared at the big old house with its boarded-up windows and the vines covering the front porch. The steps leading up to the front door looked as if they were about to cave in.

"I dare you to go up and try the door," Sam had said. When Neil hadn't said or done anything, Bob and Will called him a "scaredy-cat" and a "wimp."

And Neil was scared. Staring at the old McBride mansion had always made him feel that way. There was just something spooky about the way the bushes were all grown up around the house, the paint was peeling off, and half of the shingles were missing. People said the house was haunted. Neil didn't know if he believed that, but he was pretty sure he had seen a couple of bats flying out the roof one night.

The thought of going up and trying the door handle wasn't nearly as scary as the thought that the door might open!

Suddenly Neil found himself thinking, *But wait a minute. This isn't what God wants me to feel.* He remembered a scripture he had read just last week, *"God has not given us a spirit of fear."* He wants us to be strong and to make good choices.

"I'm not going up to the front door," Neil said. He was surprised that his voice sounded so brave. "That would be trespassing. I'm not going to trespass." He felt himself grow bolder and bolder. "And I'm sure," he said, "there's nobody inside who will invite me in and give me cookies and milk like my mother will give us."

"Cookies and milk?" Bob asked.

"What are we standing around here for?" Will said.

"Race you to my house!" Neil yelled as he began to sprint toward home.

God has not given us a spirit of fear,
but of power and of love and of a sound mind.
2 Timothy 1:7 NKJV

SAY NO TO FEAR OF WHAT OTHERS THINK ABOUT YOU.

It takes courage to stand up to a dare. Today, ask God to help you to say no to fear and no to what's wrong.

Back to the Sea

As every thread of gold is valuable,

so is every moment of time.

———— ■ ————

Steve stared into the fish bowl and sighed so loudly that his father heard him in the next room. "What's wrong?" Dad asked.

"Floaters," Steve said. "I don't have much luck with gold-fish."

Dad came into the room and took a closer look. "Hmmm. I had high hopes for those two," he said.

"Me too," Steve mumbled. "It was fun winning them at the carnival. They swam around in that plastic bag like they had a lot of life in them."

"What do you want to do?" Dad asked.

Steve thought about other goldfish in small boxes buried in several places in the backyard. "Why does God let them die, Dad? Am I killing them?"

"No," Dad said. "The Bible tells us there's a time for every-thing—even a time for goldfish to die. We don't know how long Swisher and Finn had already lived when you got them. What we do know is that you gave them a great home for a few days. They had a good place to swim, with a palm tree and castle and brigt-colored rocks. If they were swimming in the ocean, they probably would have been attacked by bigger fish."

Steve thought about that for a minute and then said, "You know, Dad, I think they'd like to go back to the ocean."

And with that, Steve and his dad scooped the fish out of the bowl and took them to the bathroom. They flushed them after a little ceremony that ended with a poem Steve had written. They said together, "God gave us life and caused us to live, two little fishes as gold as could be. We swam and we swam at our home here with Steve. And now we are headed back to the sea!"

Remember

There is a time for every event under heaven—
A time to give birth and a time to die.
Ecclesiastes 3:1–2 NASB

TRUST GOD'S TIMING.

You Can Do It!

It's hard to say good-bye to a pet, but God has a perfect time for everything in our lives and in the lives of all His creatures.

A Thanks List

This day and your life are God's gift to you: so give thanks and be joyful always!

Logan moped around all weekend—nothing seemed good enough; nothing was right; he didn't want to do anything. "Logan," Mom said, "you tell me you aren't sick, but I think you're 'sick at heart.'"

"What do you mean?" Logan said.

"A person who is sick at heart is always whining, moaning, and complaining. And that, I hate to tell you, is what you've been doing."

"I'm not whining ...," Logan said, but he knew as soon as the words were out of his mouth that they had come out in a whine!

"Are you going to punish me for being a whiner?" Logan said. "Whining isn't a sin."

"Maybe not, but whining can cause you to grow up to be a bitter old man, and nobody likes people like that. I don't want you to turn out that way, so I'm going to prescribe a cure for you. It isn't a punishment—it's a prescription."

"What is it?" Logan asked.

"Go to your room and write down 100 things you have to be thankful for," Mom said, and then she turned and walked away.

Logan knew Mom was serious. It took a while for him to get started on his list. Finally he had a list of ten things—baseball, baseball mitts, baseball bats, somebody to play baseball with, sunny days, no homework, hitting a home run, cookies, cold milk, and getting to stay up late to watch TV.

He looked at his list. "This is hard," he said.

It took Logan four days to make his list, but Mom was pleased when he handed it to her. She especially smiled when she read the last thing on his list: "A mom who doesn't want me to be a whiner."

Remember

I thank you, LORD, with all my heart.
Psalm 138:1 TEV

GOD NEVER TIRES OF HEARING YOU SAY, "THANK YOU."

You Can Do It!

No matter what kind of situation you may face, you can always be thankful that Jesus is with you, that He loves you, and that He will help you.

Included

Just because an animal is large, it doesn't mean he doesn't want kindness; however big Tigger seems to be, remember that he wants as much kindness as Roo.

———— ■ ————

"Kurt's a nerd," Boyce said. "A big ol' nerd."

"Yeah," said his friend Greg. "Just because he's two years older doesn't give him any right to say mean things to us or boss us around."

Dad overheard Boyce and Greg and said, "I couldn't help but hear you boys talking. Has Kurt been mean to you?"

"No, not really," Boyce said. "He just always puts us down, as if we don't know anything. We're just as good at some things as he is."

Dad then asked, "Do you guys secretly want to be friends with Kurt?"

"Kinda," Greg said. "He's got some really cool computer games, and it would be good to have somebody to play softball with—it's a little hard when there's only a batter and pitcher and no catcher."

"Why don't you ask him to play ball with you?" Dad asked.

Boyce answered, "He'd probably just say no."

"You don't know that unless you ask him. Maybe he's unkind

to you because he thinks you don't want him around when you don't include him in your game?"

The next afternoon the boys saw Kurt and asked him if he wanted to play some softball with them. "Well," Kurt hesitated. "Aw, come on," Greg said. "It'll give you a good chance to show us how much better you are than us." Kurt smiled and said, "okay, you asked for it."

As it turned out, Kurt was the best pitcher, but Greg was the best batter and Boyce was the best catcher. "Put the three of us on the same team and we're unbeatable," Kurt said. "You guys are pretty good."

Boyce smiled. "Just wait until you see us play video games."

Remember

The Spirit produces ... kindness.
Galatians 5:22 TEV

KINDNESS TAKES PRACTICE.

Kindness is doing something for another person—perhaps something you'd like for that person to do for you.

Someday

When God ripens apples, he isn't in a hurry and doesn't make a noise.

———— ◆ ————

"Kenny can't do anything!" Paul complained with a big sigh.

He felt he had said that a hundred times in the last two months. He could remember how excited he'd been when Mom had said she was going to have a baby. He had really wanted a brother and could hardly wait for the baby to be born. "I'll have somebody to play with," Paul had told his parents. Dad nodded and Mom smiled.

"They didn't tell me," Paul whispered under his breath at the baby in the crib, "that you wouldn't be able to do anything but cry and sleep."

"Kenny can't play with you right now," Dad said, "but just wait. It may take a year or two, but someday he'll be able to play all your games, and you might have to try really hard just to beat him."

"But how long will that take?" Paul said.

"Do you remember when Jib came to live with us last year? He was just a cute little puppy then."

"I remember," Paul said. "He was even smaller than Kenny, and now he's bigger than me."

"Right, and remember how you had to teach him how to sit up and speak for his food and how to play ball?"

Paul said, "Yeah."

"And," Dad said, "remember how you had to wait for him to catch up with you because he couldn't run as fast as you could?"

"I get it, Dad." And then Paul looked into the crib and said, "I've got a lot to teach you, Kenny. When you wake up, we'll get started. But if you think you're going to outrun me in the park like Jib does, no way."

Help the weak, be patient with everyone.
1 Thessalonians 5:14 TEV

WATCH GOD WORK IN OTHERS.

Give God plenty of time to do His work in another person's life. Nobody is perfect—everybody needs people who will be patient with him or her.

Making the Team

Prayer does not cause faith to work;
faith causes prayer to work.

——— ◆ ———

Lance worked hard all winter with his dad and older brother, so he'd be ready for baseball tryouts. One night he said to his dad as they talked before bedtime, "I've been praying and praying to make the team, but I'm not sure if God is going to answer my prayers. I don't know if I have enough faith."

"Do you believe God will help you if you make the team?" Dad asked.

"Sure!" Lance said. "God helps me all the time in practice."

"Do you believe God will help you if you don't make the team?" Dad then asked.

Lance was puzzled. "What would God need to help me do if I didn't make the team?" he asked.

Dad said, "You'd need to keep a positive attitude even if people teased you for not making the team. You'd still need to root for the guys who do make the team. Those seem like pretty hard things to do."

"Yeah," Lance said. "I don't think I could pretend that it didn't matter. Everybody knows how much I want to make the team. So I'd have to be willing to admit that I was disappointed and yet honestly be happy for the other guys."

"Do you think God would help you in all of that?"

"Yes," Lance replied after thinking about it for a few seconds. "I believe God can help me do all things—the things I want to do that are hard and the things I don't want to do that are hard."

"That's real faith," Dad said. "That's the kind of faith that will help you pray, 'Do what is best in my life, God—even if it isn't always what I want.'"

Remember

"There is nothing that God cannot do."
Luke 1:37 TEV

BELIEVE — GOD HAS JUST THE HELP YOU NEED.

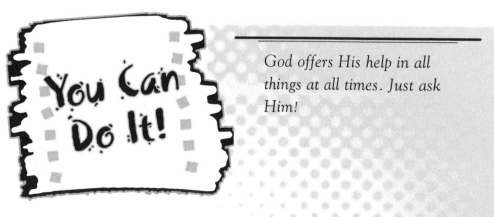

God offers His help in all things at all times. Just ask Him!

Blowing Up!

No matter how just your words may be, you ruin everything when you speak with anger.

———— ◼ ————

"I really let 'em have it," Landon said as he plopped down at the dinner table.

"I see," Dad said. "Let's thank God for the food, and then you can tell us whom you let have it."

Over dinner, Landon told his parents and sister how he had listened for two days to a class debate about whether God was real and whether God had created the world as the Bible said.

"I kept trying to speak, but nobody would let me talk," Landon said. "So right before the bell rang, I stood up and told them all that if they didn't believe in God and the Bible, they were going to hell."

"Hmm." Landon's father and mother looked at each other in silence. "That was pretty radical," his older sister said. Landon was a little confused by their reactions.

"Do you believe you changed anybody's mind by saying that?" Dad finally asked. "Probably not," Landon admitted. "But I feel better."

"Do you really?" Mom asked. "You might feel better for a couple of hours because you let off some steam, but when you go to school on Monday, will you feel better?" Landon hadn't thought about that.

That night he had trouble going to sleep. *What am I going to do or say on Monday?* he kept thinking. On Saturday morning he asked his parents for their advice. "I think you need to tell the class that you're sorry you became so angry and that you hope they'll let you give them your ideas and opinions sometime."

"But what will I say to convince them?" Landon asked.

"That's your real homework for life," Dad said with a smile. "Often our actions speak louder than our words. Others see more than they hear."

Remember

Stupid people express their anger openly,
but sensible people are patient and hold it back.
Proverbs 29:11 TEV

HOW YOU SPEAK IS JUST AS IMPORTANT AS WHAT YOU SAY.

You Can Do It!

One of the most important things you can learn is how to speak the truth without becoming angry. Ask God to help you learn this lesson!

The Recital

What a difference it would make in the world if every believer were to give himself with his whole heart to live for his fellow men!

"We're going to have a recital," Mom said.

"Who for?" Lizzy asked. Her brother Cliff and sister Jessie added, "Dad doesn't count!"

The three Harper children were homeschooled. Mom had been a second-grade teacher and also taught music. She had taught Lizzy, Cliff, and Jessie to read music, play the piano, and sing. Lizzy was learning the flute, Cliff the clarinet, and Jessie the violin. At times the house sounded like an orchestra tuning up, with each of them practicing in a different room—but Mom didn't seem to mind. She wore headphones and listened to CDs!

Mom said. "You worry about your music, and I'll worry about the audience."

On the day of the recital, Mom told each of the children to dress up in their best church clothes and be ready to leave at two o'clock. "Where are we going?" Cliff asked.

"It's a surprise," Mom said. They finally arrived at a building that looked like an apartment house. "Retirement Living," Jessie said, reading the sign. "Is our recital here?"

"Yes!" Mom said. "The people who live here are older. Some of them were musicians when they were young."

The people in the retirement home clapped loudly and tapped their toes during some of their songs, but it was when they started to sing what the children called "Grandma's songs" that the people really began to smile. It seems they knew most of Grandma's songs! One man even got up out of his wheelchair to dance.

"Recitals are fun," Lizzy said on the way home. "Yeah," Jessie added, "but only when you get your mind off being scared and watch how much fun the audience is having."

"That's true for most things in life," Mom said.

Remember

No one has ever seen God, but if we love
one another, God lives in union with us,
and his love is made perfect in us.
1 John 4:12 TEV

BE LIKE GOD — LOVE PEOPLE.

You have much to share with others—a hug, a smile, or a song. Ask God to show you what you should share with someone today.

Brent's Shovel

The secret pleasure of a generous act is
the great mind's great bribe.

———— ■ ————

Brent was itching to get outside. "Wait till later," his mom insisted. Outside the window his dad was shoveling the driveway.

"Dad doesn't look cold," Brent pointed out. "If I get the little shovel, I could help!"

"Okay. Go," she said.

"I'm almost done," Dad said, "but you can finish the last couple of feet." Brent was just warming up as he finished the last of the driveway, and he wasn't ready to go back into the house. Since the Smiths' driveway was still snow packed, Brent began clearing it. *They don't have a kid to shovel snow*, Brent thought.

Halfway down the drive, Brent began to tire, but he didn't want to leave the job unfinished. Besides, maybe they'd be so grateful they'd offer to pay him! Then he wouldn't have to wait to get the new video game he'd been saving to buy.

"That was nice," his mom said. "I know the Smiths will appreciate it." Brent wondered how much.

The snow was melting when Brent picked a quiet moment to

ask, "Dad, why didn't the Smiths say thank you for what I did? They would have had to pay somebody else to do it!"

"Is that why you did it?" Dad asked.

"Well, not at first …," Brent's voice trailed off.

"Son, when you do something for someone without expecting anything back—even a thank-you—you get the biggest reward of all."

Just then the phone rang, and the answering machine picked up. "This is Sandy Smith. Jim and I finally realized that neither of us shoveled our driveway. We suspect that one of you did, and we want to thank that person and tell him he's hired!"

Brent and his dad exchanged grins and a big hug. "Aw, Dad, I think I'll just do it for free."

"The Lord bless you. You have shown kindness."
2 Samuel 2:5 ICB

PLANT A SEED OF GENEROSITY.

Surprise someone with a kind act every day. It's a way of sharing God's love.

The Reason

Obedience is the mother of success and is wedded to safety.

———— ◆ ————

"Oops," Becca said as she stopped suddenly.

"Yeah," Brad added under his breath.

The two had been picking berries all morning. Grandpa had taught them how to pick the biggest, ripest berries and how to protect themselves from the thorns on the bushes. It was hot, hard work, but the thought of the pies Grandma was going to bake kept them going!

Grandpa had already taken their full pails back to the house, and they were working to fill two more pails by noon. Just before he left, Grandpa had told them not to cross the fence.

"Grandpa probably didn't know about those berry bushes," Becca said as she looked at several bushes filled with ripe berries just beyond the fence.

"They aren't very far across the fence," Brad said. "We could get over there and back before anybody knew."

So the two of them climbed the fence and picked berries, not noticing that they hadn't stopped with the bushes close to the fence but had moved into the pasture.

"Maybe he hasn't seen us," Becca whispered as she took a step backward. Brad also began to walk backward, and then as the huge bull took aim and began to lope toward them, they both turned and ran as fast as they could. They barely made it to the fence in time. Their pails went flying as they climbed the fence, scattering berries in a large circle.

Becca and Brad scrambled to pick up the berries as Grandpa arrived. "I see you met Reason," Grandpa said.

"Reason?" Becca asked.

"Yep," Grandpa said. "That's the name of that old bull."

Brad asked, "Why is he named Reason?"

Grandpa grinned, "He's the reason not to climb over that fence!"

Children, it is your Christian duty to obey your parents,
for this is the right thing to do.
Ephesians 6:1 TEV

OBEDIENCE KEEPS YOU SAFE.

Obeying may not be easy, and it may not always be fun—but it is ALWAYS right. Ask God to help you.

You Can Fly

Whether you think you can or think you can't, you're right.

———— ◆ ————

Will was a very young boy living in a small town in North Carolina when he began to watch the birds. Why could they fly and he couldn't? It wasn't fair. *Why would the Creator his father preached about each Sunday so favor those tiny creatures over man, His master creation?* he wondered. *People should be able to fly!* he decided.

As he grew older, he thought about finding ways to soar through the air like a bird. But it was something his father didn't like to talk about.

"Wilbur, it is impossible for men to fly like birds. Flying is reserved for the angels. Do not mention that again!" his father boomed at him. So Wilbur stopped talking to his father about his dreams and carefully hid his drawings of strange machines with wings. But Reverend Wright wasn't fooled; he could see the far-away look in his son's eyes, so from time to time, Will's father reminded his congregation that if God had meant for man to fly, He would have given him wings.

Reverend Wright was greatly relieved when Will's drawings and knack for mechanical things led him to open a successful bicycle-repair business with his brother.

But far from giving up his dream, Wilbur quietly inspired his brother with the possibility of flight. Together they studied and experimented in their shop and eventually built a contraption that looked like a bicycle with wings. And on a windy day in 1903, in a field near Kitty Hawk, North Carolina, Wilbur Wright learned that maybe God did intend for man to fly after all.

I can do all things through Christ
because he gives me strength.
Philippians 4:13 ICB

GOD BELIEVES IN YOU.

Dream your biggest dream, work as hard as you can, and trust God to be your biggest fan when the time for success finally comes!

Seeing Beneath the Surface

Men give advice; God gives guidance.

———— ■ ————

The half-hour trip inside the cabin of the boat made Nathan a little sleepy. But now the motor was silent, and Captain Jack talked on his radio to the captains of several boats drifting in the distance. The other captains said that the pod of whales they came to see was headed their way but was still several miles up the coast.

Jack started the motor again and carefully chose a spot not too close to the other boats. Silencing the engine again, he said, "Okay! You're welcome to go on deck to watch for the whales now."

Nathan rushed to the upper deck with his binoculars. Minutes passed and the boat bobbed about, but Nathan didn't see any whales. Suddenly Captain Jack appeared, swinging himself along on the outside safety rail of the deck like an acrobat. With one swift leap he jumped over the rail and onto the deck beside Nathan.

"Wow! How'd you do that?" Nathan gasped.

"Experience," came Jack's answer. "I've been on the sea nearly all my life."

"Now watch for the whales, Nathan. Three of them are coming right out there." Captain Jack pointed into the distance, but Nathan saw nothing—not even with his binoculars. Then suddenly three beautiful orcas arched gracefully through the air and back under the surface!

Nathan was astounded. Over and over, Captain Jack would point to where the whales were leaping from the water. He could see the whales approach beneath the surface of the sea.

"How do you do that?" Nathan asked.

"Experience," Captain Jack said. "Sometimes you need someone with experience to show you what's coming."

A foolish person thinks he is doing right.
But a wise person listens to advice.
Proverbs 12:15 ICB

TRUST THOSE WITH EXPERIENCE.

Listening to the advice of your parents, pastor, and teachers can help you avoid problems. They can often see beneath the surface of your life and

The Election

The strength and happiness of a man consists in finding out the way in which God is going, and going that way too.

———— ■ ————

"Are they all blank?" Angie asked as Mick began to sort through the contents of the box. "All blank," Mick said.

"Are you thinking what I'm thinking?" Mick said as he held up a stack of ballots.

This year the school election was handled a little differently. Yellow ballots were given to the students to vote for student body president, green ballots for vice president, blue ballots for secretary, and orange ballots for treasurer. The principal chose Angie and Mick to count the yellow ballots in a back room near his office and report their findings. There were three boxes of yellow ballots—but one of them was filled with unmarked ballots!

"We could make anybody we choose the president," Mick said.

"All we'd have to do is mark some blank ballots and substitute them for ballots that aren't marked the way we want." Angie added, "And throw away the old ballots."

"We'd have to hide the old ballots in our clothes," Mick said, caught up in the idea.

"Maybe we should see who won first," Angie suggested.

"Right," Mick added as he started putting the ballots into five piles, one for each candidate. When they were about half finished counting, Angie suddenly said, "What are we thinking, Mick! We can't do anything with those blanks!"

"Did you suddenly get a conscience?" Mick asked.

"No," said Angie. "I suddenly remembered I have one."

"You're right," Mick said.

Angie sighed, "Politics is a tricky business."

Five minutes later Principal Brown walked in. "Did you find an extra box of blank ballots?" he asked.

"They're right here," Angie said.

"Glad you weren't tempted," Principal Brown said with a smile as he picked them up and walked out.

Peter and the other apostles answered,
"We must obey God, not men."
Acts 5:29 TEV

GOD HONORS OBEDIENCE.

We are commanded to obey God's laws, even if nobody is watching us. Ask God to show you what He wants you to do—then do it.

A Huge Favor

It doesn't take strength to hold a grudge;

it takes strength to let go of one.

———— ■ ————

Mack loved to play ice hockey. At eleven years old, he had already decided that he would become a professional player someday, and he couldn't wait to play on a league team. He was good and everybody knew it. In fact, the coach of one of the twelve-year-old teams said he'd agree to Mack joining them a year early if all the players would vote him onto the team.

At the next practice, the coach introduced Mack to the team. "Boys, Mack can't be an automatic part of the team because he's eleven. But league rules say he can play if all of you vote to accept him. Raise your hand if you want him to play."

Most of the boys knew Mack was a great player, and hands shot up like rockets—all but one. At the end of the bench sat a scruffy-looking blond kid, and he wasn't raising his hand.

"Hey, put your hand up!" several of the boys called to him.

"Naw—ain't gonna do it. There's barely enough ice time for all of us to get to play now. We don't need him."

Mack felt like he'd been run over by a truck. He'd have to wait a whole year to play on the team.

He was still feeling down the next day in his science class when the teacher pulled him aside. "Mack," she said, "I'm assigning you a new lab partner. I know you'll help him—at least I hope so. You're his last chance. If he doesn't pass science, he's going to be held back another year. His name is James, and he's at your lab table now."

Mack turned to find the scruffy blond kid sitting at his table.

"God, help me," Mack said. He had never meant a prayer more.

Remember

If your enemy is hungry, feed him. If he is thirsty, give him a drink. ... And the Lord will reward you.
Proverbs 25:21–22 ICB

BE KIND TO YOUR ENEMIES.

Try to make peace with someone you feel has treated you wrongly—and maybe even do something nice for that person. Ask God to help you.

The Full Amount

Be true to your work, your word,
and your friend.

Danny had his first "real" job. Mr. Cotton at the take-out pizza store paid him fifteen dollars a week to hand out discount coupons to people as they passed the corner of Main and Elm. Each Tuesday and Friday Danny would hand out coupons from 4:00 to 5:00 P.M. Since Mr. Cotton paid him when he picked up his coupons at the store every Friday, Danny could go home as soon as the hour was over.

One Friday Danny dashed into the house at five minutes until 5:00 P.M. Granny Jones took note. "Danny, aren't you home a little early?" she asked.

Danny said, "I'm going to be late for a baseball game. I had to run home to get my glove. I was almost out of coupons anyway."

Granny Jones scowled but said nothing.

But on Tuesday, when Danny again arrived home early, Granny grabbed his arm as he dashed past. "Danny, sit down with me a minute—I need to ask you something." Danny sat, but not happily.

"Son, is Mr. Cotton paying you enough?"

"Sure," Danny said, "it's pretty good."

42

"And is he paying you all of what he promised?" Granny asked.

"Uh ... yes," Danny said.

"Would it be Okay if he only paid you fourteen dollars instead of fifteen one week?" she asked.

"That wouldn't be fair! He promised to pay fifteen dollars!"

"And how long did you promise you would work each day, Danny?" Danny stared at the floor. "Granny, I don't always leave early. Besides, its only five or six minutes."

"Well, Mr. Cotton could say it's only a dollar. You'd still be short, right?"

Danny thought for a second, hugged his granny, and headed out the door with his leftover coupons.

We want to do what the Lord accepts as right and
also what people think is right.
2 Corinthians 8:21 ICB

DO MORE THAN YOU HAVE TO DO.

Ask yourself often about the things you do: Are they honest and fair? Put yourself in the other person's place as you answer that question.

The Pencil

The generous man enriches himself
by giving; the miser hoards himself poor.

———— ■ ————

It was the first vacation Bible school the children in Kunda had ever attended. For forty years the Soviets had ruled the nation of Estonia, and people were often sent to prison for talking about Jesus.

Soviet times were hard. School supplies were in extremely short supply, and people had few personal possessions. Even the smallest personal item seemed a treasure. But now the Soviets were gone, and a group of Christians from America had come to hold a summer Bible school.

Speaking different languages with only one interpreter made telling the gospel story tougher, but the Americans used pictures and drama. Sometimes the room was full of people using sign language as children and teachers acted out what they wanted to say. There were crafts, Bible stories, and Bible verses to memorize in Estonian, and every day each child was given a small gift as a reminder of God's love.

One day the teacher was handing out gifts—brightly painted pencils. When she came to the last boy, her pencil box was empty.

"Wait and I'll get more," she said as she pointed toward the door. She hurried to the supply room and returned with more pencils. But when she offered the boy his pencil, he shook his head and held up half of a broken pencil. The teacher was puzzled and called the interpreter for help.

"The boys thought you had no more and were leaving," said the translator. "Olav broke his beautiful pencil and gave Stefan half because Stefan didn't have one."

Olav was one of many children who had accepted Jesus as his Savior that week. His act of sharing helped the other children see how Jesus can change your heart.

Remember

God loves the person who gives happily.
2 Corinthians 9:7 ICB

GIVE THE GIFT OF GOD'S LOVE.

You Can Do It!

What do you have that you could share with someone who really needs it? It may be your time, your help, or last year's coat. Be on the lookout for ways you can give to others.

The Great Soda Wreck

The person that loses their conscience has nothing left worth keeping.

———— ■ ————

"Corey and Candy, where in the world did you get all that soda?"

The twins' dad had glanced up from his newspaper just in time to see his children headed toward the refrigerator with armloads of soda cans.

"It was free!" Corey responded. When Corey got as far as the table, he put down his load and took a few more cans out of various pockets on his pants and jacket as his dad watched.

"Free?" his dad asked.

Candy explained as she opened the refrigerator. "There was this big wreck down on Elm Street, and a delivery truck spun around. When it did, big packs of soda pop came sliding out into the street and broke open. There was soda pop EVERYWHERE! Nobody was hurt—hardly any damage to the truck or car. But everybody started picking up all the loose cans of soda."

"Did you ask the driver if you could have the soda?"

"Well, no … not exactly."

"Then the soda wasn't free. Taking things without the owner's permission means they are stolen, not 'found,' " Dad said.

Candy's face went white. "No, Dad! Really! Everybody was doing it. Even the grown-ups!"

"When you get to heaven, you won't get to explain what all those other people did—just what you did."

Corey scowled for a second and then said to his dad, "Hey, Dad, you think you can help us find out how to return these cans of soda?" Candy added, "P-l-e-a-s-e."

Dad smiled, "Let's go!"

Remember

You might see your enemy's ox or donkey wandering away.
Then you must return it to him.
Exodus 23:4 ICB

BE A FINDER, NOT A KEEPER.

You Can Do It!

If you find something someone lost, do your best to find the owner. If you don't know for sure what to do, ask a parent or teacher to help you figure it out.

Alone with Myself

We are not at peace with others because we are not at peace with ourselves, and we are not at peace with ourselves because we are not at peace with God.

———————■———————

"You have seemed very angry these last few days," Mom said as she turned out the light for the night. "Do you know why, Drew?"

"I'm not angry," Andrew said to his mother's shadow in the doorway. Hearing the anger in his own voice, he immediately rolled over, pounded his pillow, and dropped his head into it.

I don't know how to tell Dad about the fishing pole, he thought. Dad had told him not to take that particular pole to the pond, or even out of the house—not even to show it to his best friend. The pole was too expensive. But, of course, he had taken it to the pond, and he had used it and broken it. He didn't know what would happen when Dad discovered the damage.

"God, please forgive me," Andrew prayed. "I made a big mistake. I did what Dad told me not to do, and now I've lied to Mom. Things are going from bad to worse. God, please help me."

The next morning, Andrew knew what he needed to do. He took the jar with his lawn-mowing money in it to his dad and told him what he had done. He asked him to forgive him and told him that he would save more money until he had enough to buy another pole. His father's look of disappointment pricked Andrew's heart, but as he reached for the money jar, Andrew realized that he was already beginning to feel better than he had felt in days.

Now that we have been put right with God through faith, we have peace with God through our Lord Jesus Christ.
Romans 5:1 TEV

FORGIVENESS BRINGS FREEDOM.

When you do something that you know breaks one of God's rules or your parents' rules, quickly ask for forgiveness. And then do what you can to make things right.

The Unwanted Gift

I compared notes with one of my friends who expects everything of the univers ... and I found that I begin at the other extreme, expecting nothing, and am always full of thanks for moderate goods.

———— ◼ ————

When Jonah saw the package from Aunt Florence under the Christmas tree, he just knew it was the robot he wanted. He had made a point of mentioning it to her the last time she visited.

Eagerly, he tore the wrapping paper from the box and lifted the lid.

Inside was ... not a robot. It was a bathrobe and matching pajamas.

Jonah couldn't hide his disappointment. He threw the box aside and got up to leave the room.

"Wait a minute, Jonah," Dad said, catching Jonah's arm. "Don't you like your gift? Aunt Flo remembered that your old robe has holes in it."

"Yeah, but this is Christmas!" Jonah complained. "Who wants clothes for Christmas?"

"People at homeless shelters do," Dad said quietly.

Jonah hung his head and sighed.

"I guess you're right, Dad," he said, picking up the box to take a closer look at his gift. "And I do like these. They have space-ships on them. I told Aunt Flo that I'm going to be an astronaut someday."

Dad smiled.

"I don't think you can wear pajamas in space, so maybe you should enjoy these while you can."

"In the meantime," Mom said sternly, "I think it's time to call Aunt Flo and thank her for her gift. What do you think, Jonah?"

"Will do!" Jonah said, picking up the phone. "What's her number?"

"Everyone who makes himself great will be made humble.
But the person who makes himself humble will be made great."
Luke 14:11 ICB

SHOW THANKFULNESS.

Thinking about the other person's feelings will help us remember to be thankful for whatever we receive.

Waiting for a Green Light

Wisdom is knowing what to do next;

virtue is doing it.

It was five o'clock in the morning. The sun wasn't up yet, but the Taylor family was on the road, heading to Granddad's house for Thanksgiving.

Ronny, his brother Zachary, and his sister Eve were barely awake in the backseat of the SUV. "Why do we have to leave so early?" Ronny grumbled.

"Because it's an eight-hour drive to Granddad's," his mom said. "We need to be there in time for dinner."

"And don't forget," Dad said, "that we're bringing the food. Granddad doesn't get around too well anymore, and since Grandma died last year, he needs someone to do the cooking for a big meal like this."

The streets were deserted at this early hour. It seemed strange to the children to be on what was usually a very busy road and not be sitting and waiting for other cars to move ahead or turn.

Dad approached an intersection and stopped as the traffic

light turned red.

"Why are we stopping?" Zachary asked. "There aren't any cars or any cops. Why can't we just go?"

"Because that would be breaking the law," Dad said. "The law isn't just for times when there are other people watching you."

"Laws protect us too," Mom said. "If we ran the red light and another car suddenly came along, we could be in an accident and get hurt."

"We should always do what's right, not what's convenient," Dad said. "That way, you always know what to do."

"Anyway, who wants to make tough decisions at five o'clock," Ronny said, yawning.

"I just made an easy one," Zachary said, leaning back in his seat. "I'm going back to sleep."

Remember

"Whoever obeys the law and teaches other people
to obey the law will be great in the kingdom of heaven."
Matthew 5:19 ICB

FOLLOW THE LAW.

God *wants us to do what's right, and that includes following the law—His law and the laws of our country.*

Ready or Not?

The best way to show my gratitude to God is to accept everything, even my problems, with joy.

It was the bottom of the final inning. The score was tied. The winning run was on third base. The Tigers player who was scheduled to bat next had struck out three times already in this game.

Coach Porter needed a pinch hitter. He looked at his bench. There were only two boys who hadn't batted yet: Ramon and Buck.

"Buck! You're in!" Coach said.

Ramon hung his head. He wasn't a great fielder or a great hitter, so he spent most of his time on the bench—like now.

Buck squeezed out a single, and the Tigers won, 5-4.

Ramon's dad came down to the field to congratulate him.

"I didn't do anything except watch," Ramon said glumly.

"You work just as hard as the other guys do," his dad said. "The most important thing is doing your best in practice, having fun, and making sure you're ready when Coach does put you in. It's kind of like being ready when Jesus comes back. He expects to find us doing our best, even when we're just supporting other people."

"I guess that's true," Ramon admitted. "Anyway, it's fun to hang out with my friends. And Coach always takes us out for pizza when we win."

"And you are definitely the star of this team when it comes to eating the most pizza," Dad laughed. "Let's go catch up with the other guys before they get too far ahead."

"Whoever makes himself great will be humbled,
and whoever humbles himself will be made great."
Matthew 23:12 TEV

ACCEPT YOUR ROLE ON THE TEAM.

It's hard sometimes to be a benchwarmer, but you can set a good example by being a hard worker and a true team player.

The Car Trip

Give others a piece of your heart,
not a piece of your mind.

———— ■ ————

"Are we there yet?"

Marisa, who was sitting in the backseat of the family car, had asked that question at least three times in the past hour. The five-year-old was not used to spending hours in the car. Plus, she was anxious to get to their final destination: Disney World. It was her first trip there, and she had heard all about it from one of her friends.

"Just a few more hours," said Marisa's mom from the front seat. She looked at her husband as if to say, "Drive faster!"

Marisa's older brother, Colby, was tired of hearing Marisa whine. First she was hungry. Then she was thirsty. And now she was going on and on about how long the trip was taking.

"Why don't you pipe down?" he said to Marisa. "You're bugging me."

Marisa punched him in the arm. He was about to punch her back when he heard a voice inside his head, *Do unto others*.

Where did that come from? he wondered. Then he remembered that a few weeks ago in Sunday school his teacher had talked about treating other people the way you want them to treat you. It sounded like an easy lesson then, but putting it into practice was tougher than Colby had expected.

"Hey, Marisa," he said, conquering the urge to fight back, "let's play a game. It'll make the time go faster."

"Which game?" she asked.

"This one," Colby said, pulling one of her favorite board games out of a bag on the floor and setting it up on the seat between them. "You go first."

Remember

"Your strong love for each other will prove
to the world that you are my disciples."
John 13:35 TLB

LET LOVE BE THE LEADER.

Everything goes better—even
a long car ride!—when you
treat someone with love.

A New Outlook

Prejudice is the child of ignorance.

———— ■ ————

For as long as Janine could remember, the railroad tracks divided the town's two main neighborhoods—not by design; it had just turned out that way. The poor people lived on one side of the tracks. Many of them had come to the town during what people called the "dust bowl" days.

The shopkeepers and farmers who employed them lived on the other side of the tracks. They had more money and nicer homes.

Janine lived on the "good side of the tracks," and the kids in her neighborhood regularly called the dust-bowl people "Okies" because they had come from Oklahoma.

"You can't go to the party with her," Janine said to her older brother Tim.

"Why not?" Tim asked. "She's the prettiest girl in my class. One of the smartest too."

"But she's an Okie," Janine said.

"And what does that mean?" Tim asked.

"Well, her family doesn't have as much money as we do,"

Janine said.

"She goes to our church," Tim said. "And her mother shops at our grocery store, and her father gets gasoline at our gas station."

"But she lives on the other side of the tracks," Janine said.

"Listen, Janine," Tim finally said. "I like Connie. Her folks had a hard time, but they're good people, and they're working hard to make a better life. Connie's fun and nice. As far as I'm concerned, 'Okie' stands for Outstanding Kid in Every way."

"But what will people say?" Janine said.

"It only matters what God says," Tim replied with a smile. "And by the way, Connie has a really cute brother."

There is no longer any distinction between Gentiles and Jews,
circumcised and uncircumcised, barbarians, savages,
slaves, and free, but Christ is all, Christ is in all.
Colossians 3:11 TEV

GOD LOVES ALL HIS CHILDREN.

God loves people of all races, cultures, and nations—and we are to love them too.

Keep Trying

Everything requires effort; the only thing you can achieve without it is failure.

———— ■ ————

Cameron just wasn't any good at spelling. It was his worst subject. He loved studying about things like explorers and cowboys, but spelling? He sure wouldn't win a spelling bee.

"How's it going?" asked Mr. Steiner, Cameron's English teacher, as Cameron stared at the list of definitions on his worksheet.

"Awful," Cameron moaned. "I know what the words are, like this first one: 'Animal with a trunk, eight letters.' That's an elephant. But I don't remember if it has one l or two, or if it has an *e* at the end."

"Let me share a secret with you," Mr. Steiner said. "To be a good speller, it helps to be a good reader. The more books you read and the more times you see the words, the easier it will be to learn to spell them.

"Of course, there's another secret too."

"What's that?" Cameron asked eagerly. He was hoping for

some easy way to solve all of his spelling problems, like sleeping with a book under his pillow.

"Study!" Mr. Steiner exclaimed, patting him on the shoulder. "When something is hard, you have to work harder before it starts to get easy."

"Like my model airplanes," Cameron said. "At first, I couldn't build them, but I kept trying, and my dad helped me too."

"Exactly," Mr. Steiner said. "Hard work and asking for help will put you way ahead. And it's a great feeling when you finally learn to do something you couldn't do before."

"I think I'll be ready for the next test," Cameron said confidently.

Remember

Work hard at whatever you do.
Ecclesiastes 9:10 TEV

DO THE HOMEWORK!

It would be nice if we could snap our fingers and learn everything we need to know just like that. But it takes work, and when you work at something, you really feel good when you finally get it.

Building a Castle

There are two ways of spreading light — to be the candle or the mirror that reflects it.

Keith brought pail after pail of sand to his Uncle Don, who was helping him build the best sand castle on the beach. There were lots of kids and adults taking part in the "King of the Castles" contest. Keith really wanted to win.

The sun was shining bright; a nice breeze was blowing; and Keith, whose dad had died the year before, was having a great time with his uncle.

"Keith, buddy, pack some more wet sand on that wall, so it doesn't collapse," Uncle Don said. Keith obeyed. This castle was really coming together.

Keith was working so hard on the castle, in fact, that he didn't notice another boy had walked up and was standing nearby, watching Keith and his uncle.

"Which castle is yours?" Uncle Don asked, glancing up and seeing the boy.

"None," the boy whispered. "My mom can't build 'em, and

my dad ..." The boy's voice choked, and he looked away as he rubbed tears from his eyes.

Keith looked at the boy with understanding. "Is your dad in heaven too?" he asked softly.

The boy stared at the ground and nodded.

"What's your name?" Keith asked.

"Karlin," he said.

Keith looked at his uncle, who seemed to know what he was thinking. "Why don't you help us with our castle?" Keith asked. "We'd sure like to win the contest, and I bet the three of us could build an awesome castle."

Karlin's face lit up. "Okay!" he said. "That would be great!"

"All right, you guys," Uncle Don said, rubbing his hands together. "Let's move some sand!"

Remember

Keep on loving each other as brothers.
Hebrews 13:1 NIV

PAY ATTENTION TO THE LONELY.

You Can Do It!

Think about how good it makes you feel when someone pays attention to you. Look around for someone who looks like he needs a friend, and pay attention to him.

Doing the Right Thing

What's left after all the excuses are gone is usually what's right.

"What's that mean?" Dayton asked, pointing to Michelle's bracelet.

"You've never seen a WWJD bracelet before?" Michelle asked.

"No," Dayton said. "What's it mean?"

Michelle suddenly remembered that Dayton had lived in South America, where his parents were missionaries. "WWJD bracelets are kinda old here in the United States," Michelle said, "but I still like to wear mine. WWJD stands for 'What Would Jesus Do?'"

"Why do you wear it?" Dayton asked.

"Well," Michelle said, "sometimes I don't know what to do in certain situations, or I don't know what to say—like when Chris punched Garrett in the stomach at recess today."

"That was a pretty bad scene," Dayton replied. "I saw it from across the cafeteria. What's with those two?"

"Garrett and Chris are normally friends, but Garrett took a candy bar out of Chris's lunch sack. They were both wrong—Garrett was wrong to take the candy bar, and Chris was wrong to punch him," Michelle said.

"So what would Jesus do?" Dayton asked.

Michelle said, "I think He would have done exactly what Kip did. Kip handed Chris an even bigger candy bar out of his own lunch sack and said, 'Don't be stupid. A candy bar isn't worth fighting about.'"

"You really think that's what Jesus would have done?" Dayton asked.

"Well, maybe not exactly like that, but I do think Jesus would have wanted Chris and Garrett to stay friends," Michelle said.

"I think I'd like Kip to be my friend," Dayton said.

Put all things to the test: keep what is good
and avoid every kind of evil.
1 Thessalonians 5:21–22 TEV

GOD'S WAY IS THE RIGHT WAY.

Ask Jesus any time you wonder if you're doing the right thing, "Is this what You would do?"

Stuck in the Middle

Lord, make me an instrument of Your peace.

———— ■ ————

"You have to choose," Vince said to Nolan. Both of his hands were clenched into fists, and his feet were apart in a fighting stance. His jaw was set. But Vince wasn't picking a fight with Nolan.

Vince was the leader of a group in the school called the "Hill Climbers." The group had eight boys in it, each of whom owned a mountain bike. All of the boys had blue T-shirts. Nolan owned a mountain bike, but wasn't a part of the group ... at least, not yet.

"I don't want to be a part of your group," Nolan said calmly. "I like you guys, but I also like the guys in the group you call 'Roadies.'"

The "Roadies" were another group of eight guys in the school who rode regular racing bikes. They wore red T-shirts. Nolan was fortunate to have a racing bike too, but he didn't wear a red shirt.

"But you have to choose," Vince said. "Either you're with them or you're with us."

"You make it sound as if there are only two things I can do," Nolan said. "Either join with your group or join the other group. Actually, Vince, there's a third choice and that's my choice. My choice is not to be part of either group. I'd like to be friends with all of you. I'm not going to fight you, and I'm not going to fight the other guys. And the fact is, Vince, you don't have to fight them either. There's enough pavement and off-road tracks for all of us!"

And with that, Nolan rode off–on his skateboard.

Remember

You must strive for peace with all your heart.
1 Peter 3:11 TEV

BE ON GOD'S SIDE.

Cooperation is always more peaceful and productive than competition. Seek out ways you can bring people together, rather than choosing sides.

More to Learn

Isn't it amazing that almost everyone has an opinion to offer about the Bible, and yet so few have studied it?

———— ■ ————

"I don't know why Dad makes us read the Bible and memorize verses every week. Nobody else in Sunday school class memorizes verses," Tyrone said to his sister Keesha.

"At least not every week," Keesha said.

"I heard that!" Dad said as he walked into the room and sat down at the kitchen table with them. "Are you telling me that you don't know why I have you memorize Bible verses?"

"Not really," Tyrone said. "I know you think it's good for me, but I don't really know why it's good for me. I have three Bibles I can read."

"First," Dad explained, "you'll find when you are older that you remember what you've memorized more than you remember what you just read. I want you to remember the Bible. Just like you remember the Pledge of Allegiance that you memorized, but you may not remember what you read in history class last week."

"You got that right," Keesha said.

"Second," Dad went on, "if you've memorized lots of Bible

verses, you'll have a better idea about what's really in the Bible. You are going to meet people who will tell you what the Bible says, but they have never read it for themselves, so they don't really know what it says. Sometimes people will tell you that something is in the Bible when it isn't, and sometimes they'll tell you that something isn't in the Bible when it is."

"Like what?" Tyrone asked.

"Ever heard the saying 'An apple a day keeps the doctor away'?" Dad asked.

"Sure," Keesha said. "Gram says that all the time."

"Is it in the Bible?" Dad asked as he got up and walked away.

"Is it?" Keesha asked her big brother.

"I guess we have some more reading and memorizing to do," Tyrone said.

I will repeat aloud all the laws you have given.
Psalm 119:13 TEV

LEARN TO REMEMBER GOD'S WORDS.

If you memorize one verse from the Bible every week, you'll know hundreds of verses by the time you grow up!

In Touch with What Matters

Real joy comes not from ease or riches or from praise of men, but from doing something worthwhile.

"You don't seem very happy these last few days," Mom said to Shane. "Is something the matter?"

"There's nothing to do," Shane said. "Randy and Morgan are on vacation with their parents. I'm tired of all my old video games. I'm tired of reading, and school doesn't start for two weeks."

"Sounds pretty depressing," Mom said.

"You got that right," Shane replied.

"So what are you going to do about it?" Mom asked.

"What can I do?" Shane said.

Mom reached for a recipe card from her recipe box on the counter. She wrote on it for a minute or two and then handed the card to Shane.

"Read it aloud to me," Mom said.

"Recipe for Joy," Shane read. "Think of three people you like.

Write down their names. Next to each name, write down a problem or a need that you know the person has. Pray for that problem. And then get busy doing something to help solve the problem. Make what you do a surprise."

"This will give me joy?" Shane asked.

"Guaranteed," Mom said. "When you look in your heart and do something out of love for another person, you'll feel joy."

Shane looked at the card for a few minutes and then walked to his room. He came back a few minutes later with his cap on. "Where are you going?" Mom asked.

"Mr. Phillips next door needs the gutters of his roof cleaned out, and he's too old to do it." Mom noticed that Shane was whistling and had a big smile on his face as he walked out the backdoor.

Be joyful always.
1 Thessalonians 5:16 TEV

"BE JOYFUL" IS A COMMAND!

You have the ability to choose how you will feel. If you want to feel joy, the key is to choose to help others, give to others, or share with others. Giving will cause you to overflow with joy from the inside.

Have No Fear

The only power which can resist the power of fear is the power of love.

———— ■ ————

Devon was shaking as he walked to the front of the classroom to give his speech. If there was one thing that scared him, it was standing up and talking in front of people.

It wasn't that he wasn't prepared. He had practiced at home in front of the mirror for a long time. But now his mind was blank. He couldn't remember a single word!

"Um … uh … hello, everyone," he began, hoping that the words of his speech would come back to him. "I'm … uh … going to … I mean … here's why I think people should be riding buses and trains instead of driving their cars."

He stood still and waited for the rest of the speech to come back into his mind. His hands were sweating. His knees were knocking. He could see someone in the back row whispering to his neighbor. *This is a disaster. I am doomed. I am going to get an F on my speech, and …*

A voice came from the third row.

"What's wrong with cars?" his friend Patrick asked. "Why shouldn't people just drive everywhere they want?"

"Well ... they ... there aren't enough parking places, especially downtown," Devon said, his voice growing stronger. "And you can fit more people in a bus. You can read and get work done if you take the train, and if fewer people drove their cars, there'd be less pollution."

Now Devon was back on track. As the words of his speech poured from his mouth, he noticed that he had stopped shaking. That made him smile. Before he knew it, his speech was done, and his classmates were applauding.

Back in his seat, Devon turned to Patrick.

"Thanks," he whispered. "You saved my life."

"It was nothing," Patrick said. "You did all the work. I just gave you a little nudge."

Remember

"Don't panic. I'm with you. There's no need to fear for I'm your
God. I'll give you strength. I'll help you.
I'll hold you steady, keep a firm grip on you."
Isaiah 41:10 MSG

LOOK FEAR IN THE EYE!

It's hard to do something you're afraid of. But you don't have to worry; God is always right there with you to help you get through it.

Lost and Found

I would rather walk with God in the dark
than go alone in the light.

The crowds on the dark city streets were huge. It looked like everyone had waited until December 24 to do their Christmas shopping.

"Stay with me," Martin's mom told him as they headed for a shop. "I don't want to lose you."

Martin obeyed, following his mom from store to store as she looked for just the right gifts. Outside of one store, she saw a friend from work and stopped to talk for a minute. Martin spotted some sports equipment in the window of a nearby store and went over to take a closer look. The next store had some toys he wanted to see. Pretty soon Martin realized what he had done. He hadn't stayed with his mom. He was lost!

Putting his hands in his pockets to keep them warm, he felt something round in the left pocket. Taking it out, he saw that it was a magnet he'd taken off the refrigerator that afternoon and had forgotten about. He held it up to the light. On the front, it said, "The Good Shepherd watches over His sheep."

Boy, could I use a shepherd right now! Martin thought. He

leaned his head against the window of a store and closed his eyes. "God," he prayed, "I did something dumb, but please help me find my mom. I'm cold and scared, and I want to go home."

Someone grabbed him by the arm. It was his next-door neighbor, Mr. Watson. "Martin!" he said. "Your mom is looking all over for you. Did you get lost?"

"I was lost," Martin confessed, "but I prayed for help. God sure was listening!"

"He always is," Mr. Watson said, patting Martin on the back. "Your mom is over there in front of the café. I think she said something about hot chocolate."

The LORD will keep you from all harm—
he will watch over your life.
Psalm 121:7 NIV

GOD IS ALWAYS READY
TO HELP YOU.

When we get lost, we should always pray and ask God to help us find our way back to where we belong. He really listens to our prayers, and He really cares.

Jars of Change

It's not the mountain we conquer but ourselves.

———— ■ ————

Aaron emptied his pocket and dropped two nickels and a penny in the jar by his bed. The jar was about half full. "Looking good," he said.

The jar was labeled "Sierra Leone Mission." Aaron's youth group adopted the mission school for a summer fund drive. So far the youth group had held a car wash and had sold watermelons to raise money. In addition, Pastor Rob had suggested that each person in the youth group take a jar and fill it up with the change left in his or her pocket at the end of each day.

Aaron smiled, "But Pastor Rob didn't say the change from both pockets." Aaron then emptied his other pocket and dropped a quarter into a second jar. This second jar was a much larger peanut butter jar that Aaron kept under his bed. Aaron had special plans for the money in that jar—a new CD he'd just heard.

As the time came closer for the change jars to be turned in, Aaron thought more and more about the jar under his bed. It was nearly full. "There's probably three times more money in that jar,"

Aaron said to himself. He took out a few coins and put them in the Sierra Leone Mission jar in hopes that he'd feel better ... but he didn't.

"Nobody will know," Aaron tried to convince himself. "Except the guy in the mirror," he finally added.

"Does everybody have their change jars?" Pastor Rob asked the next morning. "Yeah." Aaron said. "And some of us have two jars," he added as he plunked down not only his Sierra Leone Mission jar but also the old peanut butter jar filled with change. "I hope it's okay that I put a dollar bill in there too," he said. Inside, he knew it was more than okay.

If we do not do the good we know we should do,
we are guilty of sin.
James 4:17 TEV

LOOK FOR WAYS TO DO GOOD.

Sometimes the only two people who will know about the good things you do are you and God. But that's enough! Trust God to reward you in ways that are even better than what people can do.

A Conversation with God

When you have read the Bible, you will know
it is the word of God, because you will have
found it the key to your own heart,
your own happiness, and your duty.

"Whatcha doing?" Peter asked his big sister Hannah.

"Reading my Bible," Hannah said. She moved a pillow next to her and invited Peter to come up and sit by her. Hannah really loved her little brother, and she knew that he adored her. Even though they were five years apart in age, they had a lot of fun together.

"Are you going to be a preacher like Pastor Thomas?" Peter asked.

"No," Hannah said. "The Bible is for every person to read, even boys and girls."

"Why?" Peter asked.

"It's like having a conversation with God," Hannah said. "God wants to say something to us, so He gave us the Bible."

"Does He talk to you like my talking book?" Peter asked. Hannah smiled. Peter loved for her to read his book that had buttons for different animal sounds. Sometimes she wished God would talk to her in a voice she could hear.

"No," Hannah said. "People who heard from God in their heart wrote down what God said in this book. So when I read the Bible, it's like hearing what God has to say about different things."

"What does God tell you?" Peter asked.

"He tells me what's right and what's wrong. He tells me what's good and what's bad. He tells me how I should treat other people. He even tells me how I should treat my little brother!"

"He does?" Peter asked, his eyes wide with wonder. "What does He say?"

"He says that I'm supposed to love you and teach you to read the Bible for yourself," Hannah said. And then with a big grin she added, "And I think that means right now I should hug you and kiss you ten times in a row and then tickle you."

All Scripture is inspired by God and is useful
for teaching the truth, rebuking error, correcting faults,
and giving instruction for right living.
2 Timothy 3:16 TEV

THE BIBLE IS OUR GUIDEBOOK FOR LIFE.

If you want God's opinion on what to think, believe, feel, say, or do—go to your Bible. It has every answer you need.

Clean Talk

The foolish and wicked practice of profane cursing and swearing is a vice . . . so mean and low . . . that every person of sense and character detests and despises it.

———— ◼ ————

"I do not want you to use that word," Mom said sternly. "Never again!"

"Aw, Mom," Thomas said. "All the guys use that word."

"Do they know what that word means?" Mom asked.

"Nobody thinks about it like that," Thomas said. "It's just a word."

"Words have meanings," Mom said, "even if you speak them as if they don't."

"But everybody uses that word," Thomas said. "I hear it all the time at school. Plus, I hear adults use that word—at the mall and at football games and ..."

"Just because everybody uses a word doesn't mean it's a good word to use," Mom countered.

Then Mom sat down and asked Thomas to sit with her. "Thomas," she said, "do you think Jesus would use that word in talking to His disciples or to the people He healed?"

Thomas thought for a moment. "No, I guess not," he finally said.

"We need to learn to talk like Jesus did. I'm not saying you need to use thees and thous or talk about spiritual things all the time. But we need to talk in a way that makes people want to listen to us. Truly great people have good vocabularies, and they speak positive words that other people admire."

"I guess you're right," Thomas said.

Then Mom gave Thomas a challenge. "I challenge you to learn a new vocabulary word every day. Choose some big words and some hard words. Start using them. I guarantee that you'll get people's attention—but this time, in a good and fun way. Surprise your friends—you might be surprised in return to see how much they admire what you say."

Thomas didn't really want to admit it, but the idea sounded pretty cool.

Remember

No insults or obscene talk must ever
come from your lips.
Colossians 3:8 TEV

SPEAK AS IF YOU'RE IN FRONT OF JESUS.

The words you speak can make a difference. Choose a good vocabulary—yes, even a godly vocabulary. Memorize good words, quotes, and phrases, and learn to use them.

Heavenly Manners

He who sows courtesy reaps friendship.

—————— ■ ——————

"Why do I always have to say 'please' and 'thank you'?" Lesley complained. "And especially why do I have to say it to Bryce—he's family!"

"It's part of being polite," Mom said to her two children, who seemed to be especially eager for an argument on this particular morning.

"But why do we have to be polite?" Bryce asked. "Hardly anybody else is. Nobody is very polite in the mall or at the ballpark."

Mom decided this was the time for a serious talk. She sat down with the two at the breakfast table and said, "First of all, good manners help people who are strangers become friends. When you are nice to someone and say words like 'please' and 'thank you', you show respect to them, and in most cases, they will show respect back to you. That's the best way to build a friendship—to respect each other."

But then Mom continued, "And besides that, good manners here on earth are just practice for what we will be doing in heaven."

"We'll have to have good manners in heaven?" Bryce asked.
"Sure," Mom said.
"But what for?" Lesley asked.
"Why, to greet in a kind manner all the souls we are going to pass as we walk on the golden streets of heaven!" Mom said.

Do everything possible on your part to live
in peace with everybody.
Romans 12:18 TEV

GOOD MANNERS CREATE PEACE.

Four of the best phrases you can ever learn are "please," "thank you," "I'm sorry," and "please forgive me." Use them often!

A Real Friend

My best friend is the one who brings out the best in me.

———— ◼ ————

"I don't know why you always hang out with Marcus," Gary said to Troy. "You should hang with us. You'd be more popular."

"Marc and I have been friends since we were kids," Troy laughed. "I like hanging with him."

"But why?" Gary asked. "Marcus says some really stupid things sometimes. He's not up on anything."

"Really?" Troy said. "I hadn't noticed. What I do know is that Marc never thinks what I say is stupid. Actually, he knows some amazing things. Did you know that Marc hasn't just seen *The Lord of the Rings*, but he's read it too? And not only that, he understands all of it!"

"He dresses like a nerd."

"Who cares?" Troy said to Gary.

"But Marcus isn't really good at anything—he can't play any sports," Gary said.

"Somebody has to sit in the stands and cheer for you jocks,"

Troy said. And then he added, "And you know what, Gary? Marc would never make fun of you or anybody else the way you are making fun of him. That right there makes him a pretty cool guy."

"Well, I guess you and Marcus are two of a kind. Both losers," Gary said with a very mean tone of voice. Troy grinned. "Marc and I may be losers in your eyes, and even in the eyes of lots of kids, but I know this—he's my friend and I'm his friend. And a person who has a friend may be a loser, but he's never a loner."

Friends always show their love.
Proverbs 17:17 TEV

STAND BY YOUR FRIENDS.

Be sure to speak up when other people put down your friends!

A Little at a Time!

I am a slow walker, but I never walk backwards.

———— ◆ ————

"This tree house is going to take forever to build," Jake complained.

"Really?" Dad asked. "How long have you been working at it?"

"Almost two hours!" Jake said. "It only took Gramps and me an hour to come up with the plan, and it only took an hour to buy all the stuff I needed at the hardware store. Getting it built is going to take weeks."

"But just think," Dad said, "you'll have years to enjoy it!" Jake grinned in spite of how he felt.

Dad then said, "Good work always takes some time, Jake. God didn't make the world in a day, you know. It took a whole week!"

"Good point," Jake said. "I wonder how long it would have taken Him to build a tree house."

Dad said, "You were studying Thomas Edison in school a few weeks ago, weren't you?"

"Yes," Jake said. "He invented lots of really neat stuff."

"Right," Dad said. "Did you know that Thomas Edison had a clock on his desk, but the clock didn't have any hands on it?"

"So he couldn't tell time?" Jake asked. "What was the point of that?"

"Edison believed that work should be measured by what is accomplished, not by hours. He believed that work is only 2 percent inspiration and 98 percent perspiration," Dad said. "At the end of every day, Jake, look at what you've done—not what is still to go. If you do a little each day, pretty soon you'll have this tree house built."

And then Dad said words that were like music to Jake's ears, "And by the way, I think I forgot to tell you that Gramps is coming over this afternoon to help you."

Work hard and cheerfully at whatever you do.
Colossians 3:23 NLT

QUALITY TAKES TIME.

Even if your progress is slow or your steps are small, keep moving forward, and eventually you'll reach your goal if you don't give up.

Whose Kid Are You?

You are mine and I am yours. So be it. Amen.

"Whose kid are you?" Mom asked in a tone of voice that sounded like a cheerleader.

"I'm one of the Williams kids!" the three children in the backseat said in return, also sounding like cheerleaders.

"Who is a family?" Mom asked.

"We're a family!" the children responded.

"And what do the members of a family do?" Mom asked.

"They love one other!" the children shouted.

"Don't ever forget it," Mom said in a normal voice. "Remember that all day long."

The family said that every morning on the way to school. One day the middle Williams child—Torry—asked Mom, "Why do we do this every morning?"

Mom said, "Because I want you to know that family is very important. You belong to somebody who loves you and looks out for you. You have a brother and a sister who belong to you. You need to love them and look out for them too. And most of all, I want you to know that you are valuable!"

"Aw, Mom," Torry said. "You sound just like my Sunday school teacher. She says that same thing to us about God."

"You just gave me an idea!" Mom said. "We're going to add a line!"

"Who loves the Williams family, and who does the Williams family love?" Mom asked, again using her cheerleader voice.

"God!" the three children in the backseat shouted.

"Now—never forget that," Mom said. "Remember that all day long!"

"I will make you my own people,
and I will be your God."
Exodus 6:7 TEV

GOD IS OUR HEAVENLY FATHER— AND WE'RE HIS CHILDREN!

It is much easier to love other people when we remember that God is their heavenly Father too.

Take Time for God

Seven days without prayer makes one weak.

———— ■ ————

Phillip didn't know why, but things in his life had suddenly started to go wrong. He experienced more and more disagreements with his parents, wasn't getting along so well with his friends, and was really messing up on his school assignments. Every morning it seemed he woke up in a bad mood. It just didn't make any sense.

One afternoon while Phillip sat in his room feeling sorry for himself, his older sister Leesa came in and sat down next to him.

"How's it going?" she asked.

"Okay," Phillip said, shrugging his shoulders.

"You're having a tough time these days, huh?" Leesa said.

"Well—yeah."

"Is there something you've been forgetting to do?" she asked.

"My homework," Phillip said.

"No, I mean something more important."

"Like what?" Phillip was puzzled.

"Are you still reading your Bible and talking to God every morning? Remember how after camp last summer, you did that every morning?"

"Yeah," Phillip said. "I guess I sort of stopped."

"Maybe you should start again," Leesa suggested. "I've noticed things go better in my life when I have a quiet time every day."

Phillip knew deep inside that she was right. He needed to get back into the habit of Bible reading and prayer.

"It's easy to get busy and forget about God," Leesa said, "but He never forgets about us."

"I've just been too lazy to have a quiet time every morning," Phillip confessed. "Now that I know how bad things can get without God, I'm not going to be so lazy again. I'll start now."

I command you today to love the Lord your God.
Do what he wants you to do.
Deuteronomy 30:16 ICB

ALWAYS MAKE TIME FOR GOD.

Sometimes we get too busy— or too lazy—to spend time with God. When we pray and read our Bibles regularly, though, we have more peace, and life is easier to deal with.

Everyone Wins

It is the high and mighty who have the longest distance to fall.

Every other weekend was such a drag. Clint's stepsister, Esther, came to visit with her father. What made it worse was that Clint and Esther were the same age. What made it impossible was that Esther got As and Clint worked hard to pull Cs.

Esther was great in most subjects, but Clint also had talents. He was a whiz at the computer, and he excelled at hockey. During hockey season he lived, ate, and breathed hockey.

There was one problem, and it was a big one. If Clint didn't keep up his grades, he couldn't play hockey. Clint had a big English test next week. He had to pass or hang up his skates.

"Clint," his father said. "You need to study for your English test, so you can pass next week. English is Esther's best subject—maybe she can help." Then he left to pick Esther up for the weekend.

Things were going from bad to worse. He didn't want Esther to have a clue that he could use her help.

Esther and their father got home in time for dinner.

"Clint," Esther asked, "How's school going? Are you going to play hockey this year?"

"Sure I am," he answered. Clint suspected she knew what was up and was just rubbing it in.

"I'm struggling with computer class. I just don't get it ... I really don't," Esther said.

Clint had an idea. "Esther, let's make a deal. I'll help you with computers if you will help me pass the English test."

"Really?" Esther asked. "Wow, that would be too cool. If you help me, I know I'll be able to figure it out."

Clint was shocked that Esther needed help. *This could work for both of us!* he thought.

Remember

Be sure that you live in a way that brings honor to the Good News of Christ. Then ... I will hear that you continue strong with one purpose and that you work together as a team for the faith of the Good News.
Philippians 1:27 ICB

HELP IS ALWAYS AVAILABLE.

You Can Do It!

If you need help, swallow your pride, and admit your need. Then look for ways for your need to be met. Be willing to accept help from others.

A Team Player

Politeness is doing and saying the kindest thing in the kindest way.

———— ■ ————

Karl and his three best friends—Matty, Brian, and Theo—were on the playground at recess. It was a relief to be outside after a morning filled with math problems and a history test. Now all they wanted to do was shoot some hoops.

The playground was full of kids who were just as happy to be out of class as the four boys. Karl found the teacher who was in charge of sports equipment and took a basketball. He dribbled the ball on the blacktop as he made his way back to his friends.

Hunter came running up just as they were getting ready to start the game.

"Sorry, Hunter," Karl said. "We can't play with five."

"I'll get somebody else—then we'll have six," Hunter said, scanning the playground for another player. Spotting Sammy, he waved him over.

Sammy came limping up to the court. The brace on his leg slowed him down a little, but the smile on his face was bright.

"He can't play!" Matty complained. "He's a drag. He'll ruin

94

the game."

Sammy's smile started to fade.

"Yeah, he's too slow," Brian said. "Find somebody else."

Karl saw how miserable Sammy looked. Somehow, he knew that it was wrong to reject Sammy just because he wasn't as fast on his feet as the rest of them.

"Aw, come on," Karl said. "Let him play. I'll bet he's a great free-throw shooter."

Sammy's smile came back instantly.

"Sammy's on my team," Karl added, and was surprised at how happy those words made him feel on the inside.

Remember

"This is My commandment, that you love
one another, just as I have loved you."
John 15:12 NASB

PEOPLE ARE FAR MORE IMPORTANT THAN GAMES OR SCORES.

Always look at who a person is on the inside, not at any physical problem he might have. God looks at the inside—the heart—and so should you.

Better Safe Than Sorry

When clouds are seen,
wise men put on their coats.

If there was one thing Casey liked, it was going hiking with his dad. Early one morning after school was out for the summer, Casey's dad, who had taken the day off from work, awoke Casey and told him about their next adventure.

While Dad made his famous pancakes and eggs for breakfast, Casey put on his hiking clothes and checked his gear. They always took a compass, a map, water, a first-aid kit, and hats to protect them from the sun.

"It's going to be a great day," Dad said as they finished their meal. "The weather is supposed to be perfect."

A few hours later, as they hiked up the side of a steep hill about two miles from where they'd parked the car, Casey's dad noticed what looked like storm clouds in the distance.

"We'd better head back," Dad said.

"No!" Casey protested. "We haven't been hiking in a long

time. Let's keep going. The sun is still shining. It'll take a long time for those clouds to get over here where we are."

"A smart hiker always watches the weather," Dad said. "A storm can come up suddenly. It's better to be safe than sorry."

Dad led the way as a disappointed Casey followed him down the hill.

And Dad was right. A storm was coming–and fast. When father and son were still about twenty minutes away from the car, they heard thunder. Walking faster, they still weren't quick enough to beat the rain. By the time they reached the car, they were soaked.

Casey learned three important lessons that day–pay attention to warning signs, trust Dad's advice, and always look up.

Remember

The wise look ahead to see what is coming.
Proverbs 14:8 NLT

IT IS ALWAYS WISE TO LISTEN.

When you're having fun, you don't want anything to stop you. It's important to listen to wise advice and trust others— like your parents. Like God, they have your best interests in mind.

Dollars and Sense

A penny saved is a penny earned.

———— ■ ————

"Scott has the nicest things. He's got the best bicycle and the best computer games. He gets everything," complained Ian to his mom and dad. Although Ian was older than Scott, he hadn't learned how to handle money.

"Ian, you know that you get more allowance than Scott because you're older and do more chores," his father said. "Scott just saves more money than you do."

"Why don't you make a budget and write down every cent you earn and every cent you spend. That will help you see where your money is going," Ian's mother suggested.

"Sounds boring. But I'll do it," Ian agreed.

"Start with this week's allowance," Father said. He showed Ian how to make a chart to record how much money he had, how much money he spent, and what he spent it on. "It's easy. Just remember to write it down."

After two days Ian's father asked, "How's it going, Ian?"

"I only have six dollars after I got ten dollars for my allowance."

"Where did that money go?" Father asked.

"Well, I did get some pop after school. Then I bought two candy bars from the youth group that is raising money for missions. Oh, and I got a new pocketknife."

"Now that I can see where my money goes, I can make better choices. I can choose between a pop or saving for something nice," Ian realized aloud.

A foolish person rejects his father's correction.
But anyone who accepts correction is wise.
Proverbs 15:5 ICB

SPEND YOUR MONEY WISELY.

Save money by not spending it. Then you will have enough for what you really want.

I Dare You!

One trouble with trouble is that
it usually starts out like fun.

———— ■ ————

The old oak tree on the Myers's farm was perfect for climbing. It had branches close to the ground, and the higher branches were nice, long, and wide.

Charlie Myers invited five of his friends to come over and play. After Charlie's dad cooked some hot dogs and hamburgers on the grill, the six boys went exploring and eventually found themselves at the oak tree.

Charlie, Dennis, Gus, Macy, Jared, and Rollie quickly hopped up on the low branches and made their way to higher perches.

"Watch this!" Gus yelled. He jumped from his branch, landed on the hard-packed dirt, and dared his friends to follow his lead. They all did. Then Gus climbed up to a much higher branch, followed by his friends. Everyone jumped—except Rollie.

"It's too high!" he said. "I'll get hurt!"

"No, you won't!" Gus called. "Come on!"

Rollie closed his eyes and jumped. When he landed, he heard

something crack in his ankle. Then came waves of pain. He had broken a bone!

Later, at the hospital, his dad asked how the accident had happened. He was unhappy to hear what Rollie had done.

"Did you know that was a bad idea?" Dad asked.

"Yeah," Rollie admitted. "Something inside told me not to do it, but I didn't want to look like a wimp."

"That 'something inside' was Someone—the Lord," Dad said. "One of His jobs is to point you in the right direction when others try to talk you into doing something dangerous or wrong."

"Next time I'll listen to Him," Rollie promised. "Keeping up with my friends sure wasn't worth breaking my ankle."

Whoever spends time with wise people
will become wise. But whoever makes friends
with fools will suffer.
Proverbs 13:20 ICB

THINK BEFORE YOU LEAP.

Nobody wants to look scared in front of friends. But when you follow Jesus, your Best Friend, He will always show you the right way.

The Swimming Lesson

Courage is being scared to death ... and saddling up anyway.

———— ■ ————

"Hurry a little," Mom said to Daniel. "Grab a towel on your way out, and don't forget your flip-flops. I already have earplugs and goggles if you want them."

Daniel didn't feel like hurrying. In fact, he didn't feel like going to the swimming pool at all.

"You're acting as if you aren't excited about the first day of swimming lessons," Mom said. "You loved swimming class last year."

"That was last year," Daniel said.

"So what's so bad about this year?" Mom asked.

"This year the class is in the middle pool," Daniel said.

"Right," Mom said. "You graduated from the shallow pool and into the middle pool at the end of last summer. You learned to jump in and then float on your back and kick to the edge."

"I'm not sure I remember what I learned," Daniel said. "The middle pool is pretty deep."

"Four things," Mom said. "One, I don't think you've forgotten what you learned. It's going to come back to you. Two, your teacher will be right there—he won't let you drown. Three, you are two and a half inches taller this year. The middle pool is only three feet deep, and I think you're going to be able to touch the bottom of the middle pool this year if you stand on tiptoes—with your head OUT of the water."

Daniel hadn't thought about that. "What's number four?" he asked.

"Number four is that Jesus is going to help you do this. Learning to swim is a good thing, and Jesus always helps us learn to do good things."

"We'd better hurry," Daniel said. "I don't want to be the last one there."

"I will always be with you. I will never abandon you.
Be determined and confident."
Joshua 1:5–6 TEV

JESUS ALWAYS HELPS US DO OUR BEST.

You never know how good you can be until you try. Be brave as you take the next step toward excellence.

A Special Little Brother

From the beginning, disability taught that life could be reinvented. In fact, such an outlook was required.

When Channing was four years old, Arden was born. At first they didn't think he was going to live—he had a hole in his heart–and it was scary. But he survived the surgery, all the shots, and the medicine.

The family was celebrating Arden's fourth birthday. It was amazing. He had been so sick and now he was well … mostly. Actually, Arden was a special child. He had been born with Down's syndrome. That meant he wasn't like other children. But to Channing, he was extra special.

Arden was a delight to their family. They were closer because Arden needed extra help—and they all wanted to help Arden. It took a long time for him to walk and talk. But Channing helped him to learn.

Channing also learned a lot from Arden. He was happy. He seldom cried, and he never hit Channing. He didn't throw things or yell when she played with his toys. He liked to share whatever he had. Those were good lessons for her to learn.

Channing had to slow down to play with Arden. He couldn't walk as fast. He couldn't kick a ball very well. But he had the biggest smile whenever she played with him. He always smiled— and that made her smile too.

Even Grandma's Labrador dog liked Arden. Missy never let anyone ride on her–except Arden. She didn't care if Arden pulled on her tail or got up on her back. Missy was always kind and gentle to Arden. Somehow she knew he was a special child too.

Channing noticed that people looked at them a little differently when Arden was with them. She thought perhaps it was because they wanted a special little boy like Arden too.

Remember

Speak up for those who cannot speak for themselves.
Defend the rights of all those who have nothing.
Proverbs 31:8 ICB

EVERY PERSON HAS A GIFT.

Do you know someone with a disability? Get to know him and spend time with him, and you will be blessed!

The Ally

The song, from beginning to end,
I found again in the heart of a friend.

———— ◆ ————

"Oh no," Carlos muttered, "not again."

Brett and Dex had cornered him at his locker before. "I've got something here for you," Brett said. "You said no last time, but we decided to give you a second chance," Dex taunted as he pulled out a pack of cigarettes. "Don't let me down, Carlos," Dex added. "I've got a bet going with Brett here that you're man enough to do this."

"I don't want your cigarettes," Carlos said. "I don't smoke."

"Maybe you've been too scared to try," Brett said with a sneer.

"I don't want any," Carlos said, trying to push his way past the two boys.

"Not so fast," Brett said as he and Dex pushed Carlos up against his locker. Carlos suddenly realized he was alone in the hall—except for Adam, a boy he knew from church.

"What's happening?" Adam asked.

"We're just doing business with Carlos," Brett said.

"What's it to you?" Dex added.

"Doesn't look to me like Carlos wants to buy," Adam said. It was then that Carlos noticed that Adam was wearing a "Hall Monitor" badge.

"What about it, Carlos?"

Carlos looked down and said, "I'm going to be late for class."

"Let him go," Adam said to Brett and Dex, and to Carlos's surprise, they did! As he walked away, he heard Adam say, "Give me the pack, and I better not see you with it in school again. If I do, I'll go straight to the principal." Carlos stopped and watched as the two boys handed the cigarettes to Adam. After Brett and Dex walked away, Carlos said to Adam, "Thanks, man." Adam put his arm around Carlos's shoulder and said, "Somebody did that for me two years ago. Maybe in a couple of years you'll be in my shoes."

Remember

Two people can resist an attack that would
defeat one person alone.
Ecclesiastes 4:12 TEV

JESUS IS ALWAYS BESIDE YOU.

Trust God to send you the friends you need when you make a stand for what is right.

Life Is Like a Puzzle!

Think little goals and expect little achievements. Think big goals and win big success.

————— ◼ —————

"Hey, here's a piece. I think this one fits here. Well, almost," Alex said.

"Look for the pieces with a straight edge, so we can frame in the border of the puzzle first. That will make it easier to fill in the rest of the pieces," Dad said.

"Now let's sort the pieces by similar colors. They should belong in about the same place in the puzzle," Mom added.

On this cold and snowy night, the Marsden family was working on a big 2,000-piece puzzle—the box showed a picture of a pizza! All the pieces looked the same, but there was only one piece that was an exact fit. That meant 1,999 pieces were wrong!

"I'm glad we have plenty of popcorn and hot chocolate," Kiersten chirped. "Why are puzzles so ... well, puzzling?" Alex asked.

"That's the point," Mom said. "They are challenging. The most important point when completing a puzzle is–don't quit. We need to keep going, keep trying."

Dad added, "Every day we face puzzling situations. There are things we don't understand. There are problems that don't work out. Perhaps math is our biggest problem."

"Or grammar just doesn't make sense," Kiersten piped up. "Science? Forget it!"

"But what does it take to solve a problem?" Mom asked. "Don't quit! Keep on trying. If you have a question, ask for help. Keep on seeking and you will find!"

At just that moment Alex found a piece that fit, and the entire family gave a cheer!

Remember

"You should be strong. Don't give up, because you will get a reward for your good work."
2 Chronicles 15:7 ICB

KEEP ON KEEPING ON!

You Can Do It!

What challenging task are you tempted to quit? Do you really want to reach the goal? If you do, then don't give up, and you will find a new way to solve the problem that has you discouraged.

A Killer Disease

For a man to argue, "I do not go to church; I pray alone," is no wiser than if he should say, "I have no use for symphonies; I believe only in solo music."

———— ◆ ————

Tucker discovered something that he thought was a great way to avoid church on Sundays. He'd just tell his mother he felt sick. It wasn't that Tucker didn't enjoy Sunday school and church—it was just so hard to wake up on Sunday mornings. He wanted Sundays to be more like Saturdays.

Tucker's mother finally said to him, "I'm going to take you to the doctor to see why you're always sick on Sundays." Tucker was troubled by that decision. Perhaps he could fool the doctor too.

"Oh my," Dr. Williams said. "You are suffering from morbus sabbaticus."

"From what?" Tucker asked, with wide eyes.

"Morbus sabbaticus. It is a peculiar disease. The symptoms vary, but the disease never interferes with the appetite, and it never lasts more than twenty-four hours. The disease, however, is highly contagious. The attack comes suddenly on Sunday mornings. The patient wakes as usual, feeling fine, and eats a hearty breakfast. Then about nine o'clock the attack comes on and lasts until about noon. In the afternoon the patient is much improved and is able to take a ride, visit friends, watch television, or play outside. The patient usually eats a big supper and is able to go to school on Monday."

"It doesn't sound like a very bad disease," Tucker said.

"Oh, but it is," Dr. Williams said seriously. "In fact, it can be cause death in the end."

"Death?" he asked.

"Yes," Dr. Williams said. "Death of a person's soul."

Tucker realized that Dr. Williams knew his secret. "Oh, I get it," Tucker said. "The only thing that can cure me is going to church on Sunday."

"You guessed it," the doctor said with a smile. "See you next week at church," Dr. Williams called as he walked out the door.

"You sure will," Tucker called after him.

Let us not give up the habit of meeting together, as some are doing. Instead, let us encourage one another all the more.
Hebrews 10:25 TEV

GOING TO CHURCH PROVIDES FELLOWSHIP.

Go to church to give as much as to receive. There's somebody there who needs your smile, your friendship, your prayers, and your encouragement.

Keep Lifting!

For anything worth having one must pay the price; and the price is always work, patience, love, self-sacrifice.

———— ■ ————

Dale loved visiting his grandparents on their farm each summer. He liked finding ripe vegetables to pick in the garden, fishing in the pond, feeding the chickens and ducks, and eating fresh watermelon as well as Grandma's home cooking. He also liked to ride with his grandfather in his pickup through the fields, helping to mend fences and feed the cattle. The feeding part, however, was a little harder than he had remembered. Maybe it was because this was the first year that Grandpa had let him use the pitchfork to toss hay into the pickup and then later toss hay out of the pickup to feed the cattle.

"I'm so sore!" Dale said to his grandmother. "I don't know how Grandpa can lift those loads of hay out of the back of the truck all evening and not get sore. He's really strong!"

"Grandpa has been doing this a long time," Grandma said. "You'll build up your muscles."

Then Grandma said, "There's an old story about a young man

who went out into the field each day and picked up a newborn calf. Each day he picked it up and held it in his arms. Every day the calf's weight increased just a little, but the young man didn't notice the increase. By continuing to lift the calf day after day, the young man developed muscles that enabled him to lift the calf even after it was nearly full grown!"

"I think I'll just stick to hay!" Dale said.

"I think that's a good idea too," Grandma laughed. "But the point is that tossing hay is like a lot of things in life—if you do just a little more today than you did yesterday, you'll get stronger and stronger or better and better at the job."

Work hard and do not be lazy.
Serve the Lord with a heart full of devotion.
Romans 12:11 TEV

STICK WITH IT!

Ask God to help you complete every job you start. Ask Him to help you do a good job all the way to the finish line.

Willing to Tell

I commend my soul into the hands of God, my Creator, hoping and assuredly believing, through the only merits of Jesus Christ, my Saviour, to be made partaker of life everlasting.

Caleb and James Wood had recently moved to Williamsport, where their dad was the pastor of a church. They were a little sad that none of the boys in their new church lived nearby, but both boys began to make friends in their neighborhood.

One day James overheard Caleb talking to two of his new friends. They asked him, "What does your dad do?" When Caleb said, "He's a pastor," one boy asked him, "Are you religious?" The other boy asked directly, "Do you believe in Jeeeesus?" The boys asked their questions in a tone of voice that led James to believe that neither boy was a Christian.

Caleb responded, "I believe in God," and immediately changed the subject to sports.

James later asked his brother about the conversation. "It didn't sound as if you wanted your new friends to know that you believe in Jesus," James said.

Caleb replied, "I'm not ready for that yet."

James said, "You know, I was reading just last week about two guys named Martin." James went to his bookshelf and pulled out a book and read, "There once was a man named Martin of Basle. He was afraid to tell others he believed in Jesus, but he wrote out a letter that said, 'Holy Jesus, I acknowledge thy sufferings for me. I love thee!' Then he hid the letter behind a stone in the wall of his bedroom. His letter wasn't found for a hundred years. The other Martin was Martin Luther. He said, 'My Lord has confessed me before men. I will not shrink from confessing Him before kings.' Everybody knows Martin Luther, but who ever heard of Martin of Basle?"

Then James said, "There's a famous Caleb in the Bible, but will anybody know about Caleb Wood?"

If you suffer because you are a Christian, don't be ashamed of it,
but thank God that you bear Christ's name.
1 Peter 4:16 TEV

DON'T HIDE YOUR FAITH IN JESUS!

Never let an opportunity go by to tell people about Jesus. It may be your last opportunity—and theirs!

You Can Be a World-Changer

He who influences the thought of his times
influences the times that follow.

———— ■ ————

She was just ten years old when she began to worry about the possibility of nuclear war between her country (the United States) and the Soviet Union. So Samantha Smith decided to write to both the Soviet and U.S. presidents. It was 1982, and Samantha was an average fifth grader in Maine.

Samantha didn't know the presidents had received her letters until she was called to the principal's office one day. Thinking she must have done something wrong, she was very surprised to learn that she had a telephone call from a reporter who had learned that the Soviet president was trying to find Samantha to invite her to his nation.

Not only did Samantha go, but she also suggested that the Soviet and U.S. presidents exchange granddaughters for two weeks every year. She did this because she felt that neither president would want to bomb a country where his granddaughter might visit! Although her suggestion may not have been taken,

Samantha nevertheless became recognized as a worldwide representative for peace.

Sadly, in August 1985 Samantha and her father were killed in an airplane crash. The little girl who believed that "people can get along" was gone but not forgotten. The Soviet government issued a stamp in her honor and named a diamond, a flower, a mountain, and a planet after her. Samantha's home state made a life-size statue of Samantha and put it near the Maine state capitol in Augusta.

Samantha's mother established the Samantha Smith Foundation in October 1985 to pay for projects that teach people about peace and encourage friendships among children of all nations. She made a difference, and so can you.

Remember

"God blesses those who work for peace."
Matthew 5:9 NLT

NEVER UNDERESTIMATE YOUR ABILITY TO INSPIRE PEACE.

You Can Do It!

Make friends with people you think are very different from you, and enjoy the things that you have in common.

The Best Lessons

Learn young, learn fair; learn old, learn more.

———— ◼ ————

Harry realized one day that every time he went to visit his grandfather, he found him reading. "Why do you read all the time, Grandpa?" he asked.

Grandpa said, "I'm trying to catch up on all the things I didn't pay enough attention to when I was in school!"

Grandpa said that with a twinkle in his eye, but Harry thought he also might be a little serious. "Didn't you like school?"

"Oh, I liked school," Grandpa said. "I loved to learn. I just didn't enjoy being taught. I think I always thought I knew as much about most things as the teacher knew. It was only after I was out of school that I realized I didn't know as much as I thought I knew. And each year I seem to discover that I know even less than I thought I knew! I wish now I'd paid better attention and learned more."

"There's a lot to know," Harry said seriously. "There's new stuff all the time."

"Yes," Grandpa said. "When I was your age, nobody had even thought up the words *computer* or *cell phone*. We barely had television! But, you know, Harry, the most important things to learn never really change."

"What doesn't change?" Harry asked.

Grandpa replied, "The two most important subjects a person can ever study—how to love God and how to love other people. You can spend your whole life trying to learn how to do those two things and never learn it all."

I respect and love your commandments;
I will meditate on your instructions.
Psalm 119:48 TEV

GOD'S GREATEST LESSON IS "LOVE"!

Learn how to love God and other people. Love is not just a feeling—it is an act of giving you make with your will. Love is easy to talk about and sometimes easy to feel—but it's hard to do.

A New Game

Everyone is a potential winner. Some people are disguised as losers. Don't let their appearance fool you.

I'm so sick of playing football, Walker thought. Phil and Mike never wanted to play anything else.

Unfortunately for Walker, Phil and Mike were the only two guys his age in his neighborhood, and they both loved football. If Walker was going to be asked to play with them, it probably would have to be football.

"Have they ever tried another sport?" Dad asked.

"I doubt it," Walker said. "They eat, sleep, and think football."

"Well, why not suggest something else?" Dad asked.

"Like what?"

"Well, you really enjoyed beach volleyball a couple of months ago at camp. And you were really good at it," Dad said.

Walker grinned. "Yeah. I can spike that ball—and there's a whole lot less falling down and hitting people. There's only one problem—the beach is two hours away."

Dad said, "I've been thinking that maybe we could build a beach volleyball court in the backyard. Haul in some sand, and put up a net. Put it in that patch where the grass doesn't seem to want to grow—there'd be less yard work for me!"

Within two weeks Walker and his father had finished the court. Phil and Mike had watched a beach volleyball contest on TV with Walker, and they were so excited about the idea that they had helped build the court. And not only that, a new boy Walker's age had moved into the house on the corner!

"I'm glad Parker moved here," Phil said. "Now we can play two against two in our football games."

Walker sighed, but then felt worlds better when Mike said, "And in volleyball games."

"Guess what?" Phil added. "I was talking to Parker, and he's really into tennis too." From Walker's perspective, Saturdays were definitely looking up.

Remember

Always seek after that which is good for one another.
1 Thessalonians 5:15 NASB

BE CREATIVE IN SEEKING THE GOOD.

When you and your friends make a decision to find something you all enjoy doing, everyone will have more fun. Ask God to show you how to have win-win times with other people.

The Best Fan

The really great man is the man who makes
every man feel great.

———— ■ ————

Beau clutched the red ribbon and walked over to his parents after the soccer match. "Way to go, Beau!" Dad said. "Your team came in second in the whole league."

Mom added, "It was nice of them to give ribbons to all the boys and not just a trophy to the coach."

Beau was quiet as his parents talked to several other soccer families that had come for the final game and awards ceremony. As he walked with his parents to the van, Beau said, "I don't really deserve this."

"Why not?" Dad said. "You were part of the team."

"But I hardly ever played," Beau said. "I didn't make one goal all year."

Just at that moment Gil came over to Beau and gave him a high five. "I hope you're on my team next year," Gil said.

"Sure," Beau said, not at all sure why Gil would say such a thing. Gil was eight and Beau was only six. Gil made the most goals and was the best defender. Gil hardly ever sat on the bench.

"Hey, Beau," Gil said. "When I was six, I hardly ever got to play, but you're a good kicker, and next year you'll play more. You know what was really neat this year?"

"What?" Beau asked.

"You always yelled really loud for all of us from the bench. That was great. And you always handed me a water bottle when I came off the field. That was great too," Gil said. "Every team needs guys like you." And then before Beau could say anything, Gil ran to join his dad.

"That was nice," Mom said.

"Gil's a great soccer player," Beau said, walking a little taller and holding the ribbon a little tighter.

Remember

Encourage one another and help one another,
just as you are now doing.
1 Thessalonians 5:11 TEV

ENCOURAGE SOMEONE TODAY.

To EN-courage is to put your courage into another person. Do you know someone who is afraid? Do what you can to encourage that person!

Feeding Romper

All creatures great and small ... the Lord God made them all.

———— ■ ————

"Have you fed Romper?" Mom asked. Romper was a miniature collie the family had picked up at the animal shelter a few weeks ago. Romper had wagged his tail into the heart of every family member since then. He was a sweet, lovable puppy.

"I'll do it later," Johnny said. "I'm watching a show." He barely looked up from the TV as he spoke.

"Please feed Romper now," Mom said. "It's nearly bedtime."

"Just a few more minutes," Johnny said.

"No," Mom said. "We agreed that Romper would be fed before supper. Animals need to be able to count on their food at certain times."

"All right," Johnny said. Romper was a little more bother at times than he had counted on. Mom expected him to keep water in Romper's water dish and brush him every day. "Why do I have to do everything?" Johnny sighed as he walked past Mom with a full food dish for Romper.

When he came back, Mom said, "Johnny, let's talk a minute. You were the one who begged to have a puppy. You were the one who chose Romper at the shelter. You were the one who said, 'I'll take care of him'—even after we told you all that meant. When God gives us an animal to take care of, He expects us to take care of it, not ignore it."

"I know," Johnny said. "It's just a lot of work."

"Everything we love," Mom said, "takes work—including our relationship with every person we love." Mom then got up and gave Johnny a hug as she said, "The way you take care of Romper today is going to prepare you for taking care of other people some-day—maybe even a little boy!"

"Whoever is faithful in small matters
will be faithful in large ones."
Luke 16:10 TEV

PRACTICE NOW FOR THE FUTURE.

When you take care of a pet or do a chore regularly without being told to do it, you are showing self-discipline. That is one of the most important character traits you can develop.

Robert's Decision

Be slow of tongue and quick of eye.

───── ■ ─────

Robert was gathering up the photos for the school paper. Everyone was gone except Mrs. Compton, his adviser.

Watching from the window for his aunt's car, he noticed his friend Donald at the far side of the school parking lot. Donald had been acting weird lately—surfing the Internet and spending hours in chat rooms. He seemed lonely since his dad started working really late nights.

Last week Donald said he had met someone online. He said he felt he could talk to her about anything. Her name was Jacqueline. But when Robert and others teased him about having a new girlfriend, Donald clammed up and told them to mind their own business.

It's odd, thought Robert. Donald was supposed to be at our school paper meeting, but he wasn't. And now there he is in the parking lot. Just then a car drove up and stopped near Donald. A woman—not a girl—got out of the driver's side and came around to Donald. Robert watched as they talked for a few seconds. Finally the woman opened the car door, and Donald reluctantly got into the car.

Something just didn't look right to Robert. *What should I do? Be a busybody and a snitch as well?* Donald's mother would be furious to know he was "dating" behind her back. If he told, it could end his friendship with Donald, and he could become known as the school blabbermouth. Robert made a decision.

"Mrs. Compton, I just saw something that didn't look right ..."

Robert's quick action possibly saved Donald's life. "Jacqueline" was wanted by the police.

When Donald returned to school three days later, everyone was relieved to see him, and Donald was grateful he had a "snoopy" friend.

There are diferent ways God works in our lives,
but it is the same God who does the work through all of us.
1 Corinthians 12:6 NLT

TALK IT OUT.

Pray for your friends every day. Ask your parents or another adult what to do if you think that one of your friends is doing something that will hurt him or her.

Decisions, Decisions, Decisions

Recipe for a good life: Just add Jesus!

———■———

"Dad," Dylan said, "can I ask you something?"

"Sure, Dyl," Dad said. "You can ask me anything—anytime!"

"Everybody is always asking me what I want to be when I grow up. I told Grady at the barbershop that I want to be a fireman. But I've also told Miss Wilson that I want to be a teacher. When I'm at church, I think I might want to be a pastor, but when I'm at the doctor's office, I think I might want to be a doctor."

"Dyl," Dad said, "you don't have to make that kind of decision today. You're not even in high school yet … much less, college!"

"Well, then, why do people ask?" Dylan asked.

"I guess," Dad said, "because they are trying to find out what you're interested in. You have lots of interests, and I think that's good. The more you think about different interests, the better. You're also discovering what you're good at doing."

"You mean like skateboarding and science class?" Dylan asked.

"Yes," Dad grinned. "God has built certain abilities into you to do certain things well. As you discover those abilities, you'll know better what you want to do. Add your interests to your abilities, and you'll probably know exactly what you want to do!"

"Sounds good," Dylan said.

"The point is," Dad continued, "that you don't have to decide your future now! There's only one thing you have to decide today when it comes to what you want to be when you grow up."

"What's that?" Dylan asked.

"You need to decide that you want to be a Christian when you grow up."

"I've already decided that!" Dylan said as Dad gave him a pat on the shoulder.

Depend on the Lord. Trust him,
and he will take care of you.
Psalm 37:5 ICB

YOUR FUTURE IS IN JESUS' HANDS.

God has put at least one talent in every person. Find out what YOU are good at doing, and practice that skill. Then use it to help or bless other people.

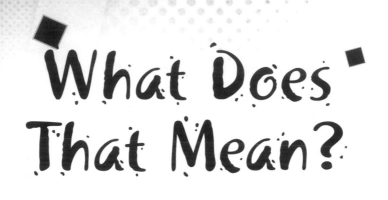

What Does That Mean?

Life is a test that has more questions than answers.

No matter how hard he tried, Ethan couldn't understand what his Spanish teacher, Senora Martes, was writing on the board—or saying. Everyone else in the class seemed to get it, but he was clueless. "Hola"—Spanish for "hello"—was just about the only word he recognized.

"Do you understand everything?" the teacher asked in Spanish.

"Si," responded a chorus of voices.

At lunch, Ethan asked his friend Dolores if she liked Spanish class. "Well," she stammered, "I don't really understand a lot of it."

"Neither do I," Ethan admitted. "I'm afraid to ask the teacher to explain it better. I don't want to look dumb."

"Me either," Dolores agreed.

At the end of class the next day, Senora Martes handed back a homework assignment. Ethan and Dolores both received poor grades. "I want to talk to the two of you for a minute," the teacher said.

As soon as the other students were gone, the teacher said, "It appears the two of you are having trouble with the assignments."

"I never can understand what you're saying," Ethan said.

"Why don't you raise your hand and ask me to repeat it?" the teacher asked.

"Because I don't know how to say that in Spanish," Ethan said. "And I don't want to look dumb."

"Would the two of you like to have a tutor?" the teacher asked. "I could put you in touch with a student from the advanced class."

Ethan and Dolores liked that idea.

"Don't ever be afraid to ask questions," Senora Martes advised. "That's how you learn. Asking doesn't mean you're dumb; it means you're smart enough to know what you don't know."

"In that case, I must be brilliant," Ethan said, and the three of them laughed.

Remember

I will tell you what to say. ... I will help both of you
know what to say and do.
Exodus 4:15 ICB

SPEAK UP!

It's impossible for people to understand everything. God is the only One who can. We can ask Him to give us understanding; we don't even need to raise our hands! All we have to do is pray.

Asking the Right Questions

The wisest man is generally he who thinks himself the least so.

———— ∎ ————

"Where'd you get that snow cone?" Jerome asked. It was a hot day at the county fair, and he'd been thinking about a snow cone for more than an hour.

"At a snow cone booth," Pete said.

"Duh…" Cal said. "We know that."

"Where's the nearest snow cone booth?" Jerome asked. "We've been walking all over the fair looking for one!"

"Well, you turn down there," Pete said, pointing past the boys toward an intersection marked by a huge popcorn machine and a corn dog stand. Cal and Jerome rushed off.

Pete sat down on a bench to eat his snow cone, and just a minute or two later Cal and Jerome came rushing up, flushed and a little angry. "I think you lied to us," Jerome said. "We went to the intersection and looked all four ways, and there's no snow cone booth."

"I didn't lie to you," Pete said. "You just rushed off before I could finish giving you the directions! It helps when you listen to the answer to your question."

"Okay, we're listening," Jerome said.

"You have to turn to the right and then go just past the Ferris wheel and turn left. There's a snow cone booth there."

Just a few minutes passed, and the boys were back. The three boys sat together slurping their snow cones.

Remember

Getting wisdom is the most important thing you can do.
Whatever else you get, get insight.
Proverbs 4:7 TEV

ASK GOD—HE KNOWS THE ANSWER.

You Can Do It!

Keep asking questions. To get the BEST answers, make sure you are asking the right questions. The ultimate right question is always, "Lord, what do You want me to do, say, or learn?"

Dumb or Smart?

Who is the wise man?
He who learns from all men.

———— ∎ ————

"Dumb, dumb, dumb," Chuck said as he opened the refrigerator door. He was surprised when he heard Dad's voice—he didn't think anyone else was in the kitchen. "Are you making up music or talking about somebody?" Dad asked.

"Hey, Dad," Chuck said as he sat down at the kitchen table and poured himself a glass of milk from the carton he'd taken from the fridge. "I'm talking about Carlton, the jerk who lives next door."

"He's dumb?" Dad asked. "Is he failing his classes in school?"

"I don't know if he's dumb in school or not," Chuck said. "What I know is that he's dumb outside of school."

"Why do you say that?" Dad asked.

"He doesn't know how to talk to people. He's always saying the wrong thing and doing jerky things. People would like him better if he wasn't always so weird."

"Sounds like you can learn from him," Dad said.

"Learn how to be dumb?" Chuck said. "Why do I want to

know that?"

"From every person you learn one of two things," Dad said. "You either learn something to do or something not to do. It sounds to me as if you are learning from Carlton some things not to do."

"I guess," Chuck said.

Then Dad continued, "It goes two ways, Chuck. You can teach a person a good thing to do or something not to do—not just in your words but also in the way you treat a person. It sounds to me as if you could help Carlton by teaching him a good thing or two. You've got a choice to make."

"What's that?" Chuck asked.

Dad finished, "You can leave Carlton dumb–or you can help make him smart."

Love wisdom, and she will make you great.
Proverbs 4:8 TEV

WISDOM IS THE KEY TO SUCCESS.

There's something you can learn from every person—and something you can teach. Make sure you are learning the best lessons and teaching what is good in God's eyes.

Show Love

There is no danger of developing eyestrain
from looking on the bright side.

William and his friend Rena were really enjoying their snow day. Rena had come to William's house that morning to build a snowman. William's mom gave them an old stocking cap, gloves, a scarf, and a carrot for the nose. Both children were convinced that their creation was the best snowman they'd ever seen.

William's mom called them inside for hot chocolate and freshly baked sugar cookies. This was turning out to be an absolutely great day.

"My mom never bakes cookies," Rena said. "We always have the store-bought kind. And she would never give me stuff to dress a snowman."

"Your mom works downtown, doesn't she?" William's mom asked.

"Yes," Rena said.

"I bet she has to get up really early to go to work," William guessed.

"Yeah, she's always gone before I leave for school. My brother has to take me to the bus stop."

"It was neat when she came and talked to our class about being a lawyer," William said. "That's what I want to be someday."

"I forgot about that," Rena said. "But I wish she was home more."

"I'm sure she'd rather spend more time with you and your brother," William's mom said, "but I always see her at your school plays. And she went with you on that class trip last month."

"I know," Rena sighed "She does lots of neat stuff for me, like singing me to sleep at night. But I wish she baked cookies like these!"

"Who says you can't bake some for her?" William's mom asked. "I think she'd really like that."

We know how much God loves us,
and we have put our trust in him.
1 John 4:16 NLT

TAKE THE LEAD IN SHOWING LOVE.

We need to realize that the people who love us have a lot going on in their lives. That doesn't mean they don't love us. And it shouldn't stop us from doing loving things for them.

The Best of Rivals

If you're for the right thing, then you do it without thinking.

———— ■ ————

Students in Mr. Brainerd's sixth-grade class were energized for the field trip to the new Porter Aquarium.

"Class, line up at the door, and we'll get on the bus." Mr. Brainerd repeated the instructions for the day. Stay in line. Stay with your buddy. No fighting or pushing. Pay attention to the guide. The children knew that misbehavior meant a loss of privileges, including playing in the soccer championship. Field Elementary could win the league for the first time ever.

Tom and Brandon stood in line together. But that didn't mean they liked each other. It just meant that both their last names started with W. In fact, the two boys were fierce soccer competitors. Actually, Tom was jealous of Brandon's passing ability, but he would never let Brandon know it. Brandon admired Tom's quick running, but he would never admit it.

Inside the aquarium, students lined up to view the fish tanks. Jeremy wasn't watching where he was walking. He tripped over a bench, pushing Brandon and knocking him into the trash can.

138

Mr. Brainerd spotted Brandon at the bottom of the heap and asked, "What happened?"

No one spoke. Jeremy was both a klutz and a bully. If you said something that got him in trouble, that meant trouble for you!

Jeremy said, "Brandon pushed me."

Tom knew that wasn't true. He saw the whole thing. What should he do? Keep silent? Go along with the accuser? Defend his rival? If Brandon got in trouble, that meant he was out of the soccer game. Tom spoke up, "Brandon didn't do it. Jeremy wasn't watching where he was going." Students near the heap agreed.

"Jeremy, is that true?" Mr. Brainerd asked.

"Yes, sir," replied Jeremy, realizing there were eyewitnesses.

"Hey, Tom, thanks," Brandon said. "We make a great team."

It is our own face that you see reflected in the water
and it is your own self that you see in your heart.
Proverbs 27:19 TEV

PRACTICE MAKES PERFECT.

Practice doing the right thing, and then when you are in a difficult situation, doing the right thing will come naturally.

Kindness Counts

The only time to look down on your neighbor
is when you are bending over to help.

———— ■ ————

Daphne and Gregory were in the backyard playing badminton. Their mom asked them to go outside and play while she finished some reports from her office.

A few minutes after the two of them started their game, Clifton from next door came through the gate.

"Hi!" he said.

"Not him again," Gregory muttered under his breath.

For once, Daphne agreed with her brother.

"Hi, Clifton," she said. "I'm really sorry, but Gregory and I have to go in now. Our mom needs us to do something for her. We'll see you later." She and Gregory walked away. Clifton stood alone in the yard, looking very sad.

Mom was standing at the sink when Daphne and Gregory came in.

"Why didn't you invite Clifton in?" she asked.

"He's always coming over," Daphne complained.

"I'm tired of playing with him," Gregory added.

"I think you should be nicer to him," Mom said. "You know that his parents are getting a divorce. Clifton doesn't know which one of them he will be living with. I think he's probably lonely and confused and feeling unloved. I think he could really use a friend right now."

Daphne and Gregory felt ashamed of their behavior.

"Let's ask Clifton to come over for dinner, okay?" Mom asked.

"Okay," Daphne agreed. "Can we make some brownies for dessert? I know he likes those."

"And after dinner," Gregory said, "Clifton and I can play with those walkie-talkies Dad gave me for my birthday."

It is a sin to hate your neighbor.
But being kind to the needy brings happiness.
Proverbs 14:21 ICB

KINDNESS COUNTS.

How do you think Jesus would treat your next-door neighbor? Would He get bored with him and tell him to go away or avoid him? No. Treat your neighbors the way Jesus would treat them.

A Winning Attitude

If you've anything to do,
do it with all your might.

——— ———

The Brady Blue Jays faced their stiffest competition, the Jefferson Jets, in the finals for a chance to go to the tournament. The Blue Jays had a great baseball season with their new coach.

The score was 4-3 in the bottom of the ninth inning, with the Blue Jays behind. Garrett was at bat. Sean was leading off second base, so he could go for third as soon as the ball was in play. He knew Garrett could hit a home run. That gave Sean a chance to tie the game with Garrett making the winning run.

What a moment for these close friends. Their hearts were set on winning. And in this moment they knew they could make it happen for the Blue Jays!

The pitcher threw the ball. Garrett was ready. Sean heard the crack of the bat as the ball sailed into center field.

Sean was almost to third and saw Coach motion him to home plate. He rounded third and went for home. The ball was coming in from the outfield. Sean slid into home. It was close … very close ... too close. Sean looked up right as the umpire yelled, "Out!"

"No way!" Sean stormed. "I was safe."

The game was over. The Blue Jays had lost.

The Jets were ecstatic. Garrett ran off the field to Sean.

"Wow, Sean! I've never seen you take the bases like that! You were awesome!"

"But we lost."

"But we played our best game ever—and you were great! Coach motioned you to run to home. That was our only chance."

"I thought I let the team down."

"No way, Sean. You played your best! We can take the Jets next season."

Remember

"God does not see the same way people see. People look at the outside of a person, but the Lord looks at the heart."
1 Samuel 16:7 ICB

WINNERS DO THEIR BEST
NO MATTER WHAT!

You Can Do It!

Put your full energy into the things you want to achieve. A halfhearted effort rarely wins.

Someone Worth Copying

Children have more need of models than of critics.

The funeral for Madison's grandfather was one of the biggest the town had ever seen. More than 500 people came to the church for the memorial service. Friends of Granddad who had known him since childhood, neighbors, people he'd worked with, younger friends, shopkeepers, siblings, his children and grandchildren—they all came to celebrate the life he had lived. Madison had no idea that his granddad had known so many people!

"We're here today to say good-bye to a dear friend," the minister said as the service began. "The good news is, it's not really good-bye. It's more like, 'See you later, Floyd,' because we know that Floyd is in heaven with our Lord, and we know we'll see him again when we all get up there."

When the minister finished speaking, several of Granddad's friends and relatives got up to talk about how special he had been. They told story after story about the times he loaned them money, helped shovel snow from their driveways, jump-started their cars, gave them rides to the airport, and comforted them when their loved ones died—it seemed as if Granddad had stopped at nothing to show God's love to the people in his life.

"The best thing I can say about my dad," Madison's dad added, "is that I am a better person because my dad was a loving, compassionate, honest, forgiving man; and I always wanted to be just like him."

"You know what, Dad?" Madison asked when the service ended. "After hearing all those people say all those great things about Granddad, I've decided that I want to be just like him too."

Follow God's example in everything you do,
because you are his dear children.
Ephesians 5:1 NLT

FOLLOW THE EXAMPLE OF JESUS.

It's wonderful to try to be like people who are setting a good example for us. But the best example we've ever had is Jesus. If we can be like Him, we will really be something!

Words Count

Words can destroy. What we call each other ultimately becomes what we think of each other, and it matters.

Ben and the other guys in his class waited in the gymnasium for basketball practice to start. They hadn't met the new coach yet, but they had heard he was great and had just coached a team to a tournament championship. They were excited—anticipating a great new season with a great new coach.

The guys chattered as they waited. Drew told a joke he had overheard his father tell. A couple of guys laughed–but not Ben. He was uncomfortable. The joke included some bad names for particular races of people. Ben didn't know if he should say something or ignore it. It didn't really hurt anybody, did it?

"Be careful what you call people. Even if they don't know what you said," Ben heard himself saying.

"It was just a joke, Ben. I was just having a little fun."

"It makes a difference how you talk about other people. The way you talk about people is how you will treat them."

"Get over it. Lots of people use the same words. You hear it all the time."

"That doesn't make it right. We shouldn't make fun of people—no matter who they are."

"Are you too good for us, Ben?"

"That's not the point, Drew. We all need to laugh, but we should never laugh at someone else's expense."

Drew's back was to the door as Principal McKinney walked in with the new coach.

"Sorry we're late, guys," Principal McKinney said. "Meet your new coach–Coach Rodriguez. He moved here from Chile where he coached a fifth-grade team to the Santiago city championship. We're really lucky to have him at McLain Elementary."

Drew looked surprised. He leaned over to Ben. "You're right. I'm sorry for laughing at people I know nothing about."

Remember

If there were a person who never said
anything wrong, he would be perfect.
He would be able to control his whole body, too.
James 3:2 ICB

WORDS BECOME ACTIONS.

Reach out to a person of a different nationality. Ask that person about his or her family and things the family likes to do together. You might be surprised by what you learn.

Do Not Enter

The way out of trouble is never as simple as the way in.

The warehouse on the outskirts of town had been boarded up for years. There were padlocks on all the doors and No Trespassing signs everywhere. Jackson and Amber passed it every day on their way to school.

Jackson and his sister were new in town. They had moved to Sundale in early August. Eager to fit in, they were happy when K. J., one of the boys in Jackson's class, asked them to walk home from school with him and his friends.

As they came to the warehouse, K. J. said, "I know a way to get in there. Let's go check it out."

"Yeah, let's do it," Terese said.

"But the signs say No Trespassing," Amber protested.

"You're not afraid, are you?" one of the boys teased her.

"We'd be breaking the law," Jackson said, defending his sister.

"There are no cops around," Bobby offered. "No one will know."

"We'll all know we did something wrong," Amber said.

"I'm going in," K. J. said "Anybody else coming?"

"Sure, I'm not scared," Bobby said, making a face at Amber. Everyone except Jackson and Amber went with him.

Moments later alarms went off. Jackson and Amber watched as five scared kids were escorted out of the building by a security guard who patrolled the lot. "No! Don't call my parents!" they heard Terese cry.

"I'm glad we didn't go in there," Amber said as they headed home.

"Me too," Jackson said. "I want to make friends, but not the kind who will get us into trouble."

Remember

"Those who claim they belong to the Lord must turn away from all wickedness."
2 Timothy 2:19 NLT

AVOID TROUBLE!

God wants you, as a Christian, to set a good example for other people. You can be a leader. You can stand up for what's right, no matter how old you are.

The Open Gate

[God] can hear everybody at the same time, because He is the good heavenly Father, and not a mere mortal like you and me.

———— ■ ————

"Emergency! Somebody call 9-1-1! There's been an accident!" Kevin yelled.

Kevin's mom ran out of the house. Neighbors rushed down the street. A motorcycle rider had swerved to avoid a deep pothole and hit a parked car.

Mr. Sanders helped the injured driver until the ambulance arrived. He didn't seem seriously injured, but he needed to go to the hospital. The medics loaded him into the ambulance and took off, sirens screaming.

"Let's pray that that man will be all right."

"Good idea, Kevin," his mother said.

They prayed together, and Kevin headed to the backyard to his dog, Princess. Uh-oh. Kevin had left the yard gate open when he ran to the street. Surely Princess was still there. He called, "Princess! Come here, girl!" But Princess was missing.

She couldn't have gone far. Kevin and his dad went down the block calling her name. They went door to door asking if anyone had seen Princess. They called the police and the animal shelter to report their lost pet.

"It's getting late, Kevin. We'll look again tomorrow," his dad said. "Let's pray that we'll find Princess."

Kevin prayed, "Dear Lord, keep Princess safe and help us find her soon."

Kevin and his dad saw someone standing outside their house with a dog in his arms. Could it be Princess?

Princess freed herself from her finder's arms and ran to Kevin.

"We found her on our block," the boy said. "We were afraid she would get run over, so we put her in the house until Dad got home to help us find her owners."

Kevin reached his arms out to Princess. "Princess, I'm sorry I left the gate open. It will never happen again!"

I pray that the God who gives hope will fill you with much joy and peace while you trust in him.

Romans 15:13 ICB

GOD CARES ABOUT EVERYTHING.

Ask God to help you take care of someone who is counting on you.

Service with a Smile

When it is possible, we should show courtesy to everyone, if we wish it to be
extended to us in our hour of need.

———— ◼ ————

"You cut the grass too close, and it will die in this heat," Mr. Grable said as he handed the money to Kale. Kale made a quick exit. He was thankful for the money he earned cutting Mr. Grable's lawn, even if Mr. Grable was hard to please.

Mr. Grable had been their neighbor all of Kale's life. He had been there when Kale broke his arm learning to skateboard. He had watched for cars as the kids got off the school bus and crossed the street. But lately Mr. Grable hadn't been doing well.

When Kale got home, he complained to his dad. "I can't do anything right for him."

Dad agreed that Mr. Grable was unhappy, "His life has become difficult."

Monday morning Kale was late getting up for school. His mother helped him find the books to return to the library. He didn't have time for breakfast, so Mom put a muffin in his lunch bag for him to eat on the way to school. "Where are my tennis shoes?" Kale shouted. "I need them for practice."

They got everything together, and Dad and Kale left in the car. Kale looked in his lunch bag for the muffin his mother had put there, "Yuk. I don't like blueberry. I wanted a banana muffin," Kale complained.

Kale reached for his book bag as they got close to school. Dad said, "Kale, your mother didn't have to help you get ready for school today. That's your responsibility. Did you say thank you?"

Kale realized he had forgotten. It wasn't her fault that he was late.

"Remember how you felt about Mr. Grable? It doesn't feel good if your efforts aren't appreciated."

"I'm sorry, Dad. I realize that I made things difficult this morning. I'll thank Mom when I get home today."

"I will make you wise. I will show you where to go.
I will guide you and watch over you."
Psalm 32:8 ICB

EVERYBODY NEEDS TO BE APPRECIATED.

Say "thank you" to someone who helps you every day. By thanking others, you thank God for providing others to do for you what you can't do for yourself.

Honor Your Parents

Respect is love in plain clothes.

———————— ■ ————————

Mishi, Nia, and their dad had been invited to a Fourth of July cookout at Micah's house. About ten families came to enjoy the sunshine, the pool, and some good food.

As the afternoon wore on, some of the dads played horseshoes while the kids played tag, and the moms made sure the food and ice didn't run out.

Micah, who was hot and sweaty from running, came dashing up to his mom and demanded a Popsicle.

"Just a minute," his mom said. "I need to finish dishing out this salad."

"Now!" Micah demanded loudly. "I want a Popsicle now, not later!"

"Keep your voice down," Micah's mom said.

"No!" Micah yelled, stomping his foot. "Get it for me now!"

Micah's mom gave him a look and told him to come with her into the house. She returned a few minutes later and said that Micah would be staying in his room for a while.

"Poor Micah missed the rest of the party," Mishi said.

"I think she should have just yelled at him," Nia said.

"Or given him the Popsicle," Mishi said.

"Do you think Micah deserved the Popsicle?" Dad asked. "It seems to me he was being very disrespectful."

"But it was a party!" Mishi said. "And he was hot."

"That doesn't give anyone the right to be disrespectful or rude," Dad said. "You should always be polite to other people—especially your parents. If you can't respect the most important people in your life, you'll never learn how to respect strangers. And, believe me, showing respect will make you a lot more popular than being rude."

"And you'll spend less time in your room," Nia said.

Remember

"Honor your father and your mother. The Lord your God has commanded you to do this. Then you will live a long time. And things will go well for you in the land."
Deuteronomy 5:16 ICB

RESPECT BRINGS GREAT REWARDS.

You Can Do It!

Now is the best time to honor your parents and show proper respect for them. There is no time off from treating your parents the way that God expects you to treat them. Be respectful!

Bikes and Bullies

Sooner or later, the truth comes to light.

———— ■ ————

"Dad, I think I'll go cut the grass," Riley said.

That was a surprising offer from Riley on a Saturday morning. Riley's dad wondered what was up, but he had a nine o'clock tee time and had to be on his way.

"Sure. Thanks! I can do the edging when I get back. Let's do something fun together this afternoon."

Riley wanted to be sure his dad didn't see his bike, so he had put it in the backyard instead of in the garage when he got home from school Friday. He offered to mow the lawn to keep his dad out of the backyard.

Riley had gone to the park when he was supposed to be at a club meeting. He had parked his bike by the creek, and some bullies broke the wheel spokes. Now he had to replace them before anyone found out—especially his dad.

With this week's allowance, Riley had enough money to buy new spokes. He planned to stop by the bicycle shop on his way home from school on Monday.

Riley bought the spokes after school on Monday. When he

got home, he went to the backyard to get his bike.

What a surprise! The wheel spokes were already fixed.

His dad met him in the backyard. "Dad, about my bike ...," Riley said.

"I fixed it yesterday when you were at Graham's. Do you want to tell me what happened?"

Riley poured out the whole story. "I'm sorry, Dad. I should have told you the truth right away."

"Riley, you can always come and talk to me. I want you to tell me the truth—no matter what. Disobedience makes you want to cover up, but the truth brings everything out in the open."

Remember

"You will know the truth,
and the truth will set you free."
John 8:32 TEV

YOUR PARENTS ARE YOUR BEST
FRIENDS.

You Can Do It!

Take time today to share your worries with your mother or father or another adult you can trust. They want to help you find a solution.

Taking a Collection

Trust God for great things. With your five loaves and two fishes, he will show you a way to feed thousands.

———— ■ ————

It was a few weeks after Alston and his twin sister, Adela, had returned to school following summer vacation. Alston looked at the calendar and became depressed.

"What's wrong with you?" asked Adela, who noticed that he seemed unhappy.

"It's two whole months until Thanksgiving," Alston said gloomily, "and three whole months until Christmas. I know we have that All Saints' party at church in November, but I need something to think about now besides just school and homework and tests."

"Let me see that calendar," Adela said. She had to admit there wasn't much happening in October.

"Do you realize how the two of you sound?" their mother asked. "All you can think about are holidays! You need to think about something else."

"Like what?" Alston asked.

"Like other people. If you really want something to do in

October, why don't you do something for World Food Day? It's on October 16."

"What can we do?" Adela asked.

"Maybe you could collect canned goods for the local food bank," Mom said.

Alston thought for a minute. "We could tell the people at church what we're doing and ask them to bring stuff on Sundays."

"Maybe the principal would let us make an announcement at school," Adela suggested.

"I bet our neighbors would help too," Alston said.

"Dad and I can pick up and deliver the food," Mom offered.

"This will be fun," Alston said.

"And we'll be helping a lot of hungry people," Adela said. "That's the best part."

Remember

If you help the poor, you are lending to the LORD—
and he will repay you!
Proverbs 19:17 NLT

OFFER YOUR HELP.

Instead of thinking about fun things you can do for yourself, take time to think about things you can do for others. You'll be surprised what a difference you can make in someone's life.

War Heroes

Hug [your] grandparents and say, "I want to thank you for what you've done to make me and my life possible."

"Derek hit me!"

"Norris punched me!"

"Derek took my video game."

"Norris wouldn't let me on the computer."

The track meet had been canceled because of bad weather, and the twins were disappointed. Who wanted to stay inside on a Saturday?

"Derek and Norris, no arguing." Dad shared their disappointment, but he was tired of listening to them. "I need your help cleaning the basement."

Oh no. Derek and Norris looked at each other. They had gone too far. They made their way to the basement. Boxes were everywhere. This would be a long afternoon.

Their job was to sort things into piles—all the tools in one place; camping gear in another; suitcases in the corner; sports equipment by the stairs; games, puzzles, and Christmas decorations on the shelves.

In sorting through the boxes, Derek uncovered an old trunk.

"What's in here?" he asked. The trunk was locked.

Dad took a look. "Why, it's Gramps's army trunk. I wondered what happened to it." He loosened the lock with a pocketknife.

"What's all this?" Norris asked.

An army uniform, blanket, and helmet, old letters and maps, medals, a ration pack, and other memorabilia from World War II held secrets for the boys from Grandpa's past.

The boys carefully unpacked each item. As they did, Dad recalled the adventures he had heard his own father tell about when Gramps had been a prisoner of war.

Then Mom called from upstairs, "What do you want for supper?"

"Let's pick up Gramps and take him to his favorite restaurant," the boys suggested. They all agreed.

Encourage each other every day.
Hebrews 3:13 ICB

POUR OUT SOME SUNSHINE TODAY.

Share some time today with someone who would enjoy your company. Ask that person to tell you his or her favorite things.

Bad Idea

Right is right, even if everyone is against it; and wrong is wrong, even if everyone is for it.

Marshall thought the school day would never end. He had received an invitation to go to Zoey's house with a bunch of other kids to listen to music. Zoey had a great CD collection.

The final bell finally rang. Marshall and the others rode their bikes to Zoey's. They each chose their favorite sodas from the basement refrigerator and flopped down in the overstuffed couches and chairs. The music Zoey selected was terrific, and everyone was soon having a great time.

At one point Zoey ran upstairs and came back down with something hidden behind her back.

"Anybody want to try some of this?" she asked, showing them a bottle of wine.

"Zoey! Your mom's going to kill you!" squealed one of the kids.

"She's not home yet," Zoey said. "She called and said she'd be late."

"We still can't drink that," Marshall said.

"Why not?" Zoey demanded.

"Because," Marshall said, "we're too young, it's illegal, it's bad for us, and our parents have all told us not to."

"Our parents will never know," Zoey said.

"Yes, they will," one girl said. "My mom always knows when I've done something wrong."

"You guys are no fun," Zoey pouted.

"What's fun about breaking the rules, getting sick, and getting caught and punished?" Marshall asked.

"Marshall's right," another boy said. "Doing something on purpose that could get you into trouble is just plain stupid. And as my dad says, he's not raising stupid kids."

"Okay, fine," Zoey said. "Maybe you're right. I don't want to get yelled at either."

Continue in the truths that you were taught and firmly believe.
2 Timothy 3:14 TEV

STAND UP FOR WHAT YOU BELIEVE.

Do what's right just because it's right. Somewhere along the way, you'll find your reward was in the doing.

Two Heads Are Better than One

From the time we were children, my brother Orville and myself lived together, played together, worked together and, in fact, thought together.

———— ■ ————

"We can figure this out ... somehow," Josh said.

"There's got to be a way," Timothy agreed.

They were still short of funds.

The brothers were plotting how to get a Christmas gift for their mother and father. They had put a DVD player on layaway, thinking they would have enough money to get it out by Christmas. But they didn't. Christmas was only six weeks away.

"Maybe we can take out a loan," Josh offered.

"I don't know if we could—and I don't think Dad would want us to do that."

The two mulled over their dilemma and decided, "Let's keep thinking."

"Come on, boys. Let's get groceries and take them to Grandma," Mom was at the door ready to go.

Grandma Branson was at home with nursing care, after having broken her hip. She was improving, but still couldn't get out to buy groceries. Timothy and Josh did the shopping with Mom and then drove over to Grandma's house.

"Thanks, boys," Grandma said. "This is a real treat to have you bring my groceries. You don't know how much this means to me. I have some other friends who could use helpers like you."

Josh and Timothy looked at one another with the same idea at the same time. They could start a grocery delivery service for Grandma's friends. They would charge a small fee, and by Christmas they would have enough to get the DVD player out of layaway.

"Grams, we would love to do that! If you'll give us the names of some of your friends, we'll contact them."

"That's a great idea, boys. My address book is in the desk. I'll tell them to give you their business."

Two people are better than one.
They get more done working together.
Ecclesiastes 4:9 ICB

PROBLEMS ARE OPPORTUNITIES.

Does something look impossible to you today? Ask for help from someone you trust and respect. Ask God to show you the best possible solution.

A Reason for Everything

People see God every day; they just don't recognize Him.

— ◼ —

Todd and Carrie set out with their mom for their favorite restaurant. Their dad was out of town, and Mom's car was getting repaired. Mom often treated the kids to dinner out when Dad was away.

"We can walk," Todd had said. "The restaurant is only about twelve blocks away."

"Okay, kids. Let's give it a go!"

"Hurray!" Todd and Carrie shouted.

It took longer than they thought, but they all stayed together and kept on.

"I can see the sign. Only two more blocks and we're there, Carrie. You can do it!"

And they did! The restaurant was crowded, and the order took longer than usual, but it tasted great!

After dinner they started for home. It was late, and Carrie was tired after the long walk there. She finally just sat down on the sidewalk and started to cry.

"Let's pray, kids, that we will get a ride home," Mom said.

And they did.

Within minutes a neighbor drove by and noticed the Grissoms. "Hey, do you need a ride?"

"Yes, thanks!" Mrs. Grissom said.

"Hop in."

"Mrs. Jackson, Carrie got too tired to walk home, so we prayed for a ride. It wasn't long before you came along in the car," Todd said.

"Really? Is that so?" Mrs. Jackson replied.

"I can't wait to tell my Sunday school class," Todd replied. "Mrs. Jackson, do you want to come to church with us?"

Mrs. Jackson and her husband never went to church, but now she thought it might be a good idea.

"Why sure, Todd," she said. "Mr. Jackson and I would love to go with you."

Remember

"If you ask for anything in my name, I will do it for you. Then the Father's glory will be shown through the Son."
John 14:13 ICB

PRAY ABOUT EVERYTHING.

Share a prayer—and then share the answer. God will use it to bless others.

The Storm

Anger itself does more harm than the
condition which aroused anger.

———— ◼ ————

Kirby had waited all week for today. He and his best buddy, Austin, had collected all kinds of containers to use as molds for their sand castle. They had even sketched out just how it would look. This year, they agreed, they would win the prize for the best sand castle in their age group!

They arrived at the beach early, staked out a great spot, and set to work. Kids of all ages were building sand castles. Kirby and Austin's castle rose quickly, and it was magnificent.

Kirby had just turned the last pointy paper cup of sand upside down to finish off a turret when a boy chasing a much larger boy ran toward them. Just as the larger boy reached the castle, he made a great leap and jumped all the way over it. But the second boy's legs were not as long, and when he leapt across, the tallest tower came tumbling down, smashing part of a lower wall with it. To make it worse, both boys laughed as they continued to run away. Austin was stunned, but a flash of anger swept across Kirby's face.

"NO! NO! NO!" he screamed. "Why? Why?" And with that, he took one of the large pails and began swinging at the castle as he continued to scream. Sand flew everywhere, and in only seconds the beautiful castle disappeared into the beach.

"Kirby!" Austin yelled. "We could have fixed it! Ah, man!" And with that, Austin stalked off.

Austin's mom, who had brought the boys to the beach, came and sat down by Kirby.

"Kirby," she said, "when you let your anger tell you what to do, nobody wins—least of all you. In the end, Kirby, your anger destroyed the castle—not those boys."

Remember

A person who quickly gets angry causes trouble.
But a person who controls his temper stops a quarrel.
Proverbs 15:18 ICB

CONTROL YOUR ANGER.

You Can Do It!

When someone makes you angry, count to ten before you act or speak. Ask God to help you keep from responding in anger.

Shared Grandparents

[My grandmother] taught me early on about doing the right thing, working hard, doing a job well, and having fun.

———— ∎ ————

"David! Abbie! Cameron! Come to the house, please!" Dad called to the children in the backyard.

It was a beautiful fall Saturday, and they were enjoying the outdoors.

"Your grandparents called and need help moving their deck furniture into the garage. They'll be leaving soon for Florida for the winter, and they need to get this done. I told them we would be over this afternoon."

The kids loved their grandparents, but they had other plans. "I was going fishing with Joseph," Cameron whined.

"Angela and I were going to ride bikes this afternoon," Abbie responded.

The youngest, David, was not yet in school. "Dad, I can help. I'll do it with you!"

"Thanks, David," he said, "Now, how about you two?"

"I guess we can fish some other time," Cameron said. Abbie

was not eager to give up her bike ride, but she said, "Well, okay. I'll call Angela."

"Thanks, kids. Maybe your friends would want to join us. It won't take long."

Mr. and Mrs. Stebbins loaded the kids, and on the way they picked up Angela.

The chore only took an hour with all of them working together. Afterward Grandma and Grandpa had hot cider and popcorn ready. "Thanks a lot, kids," Grandpa said. "We couldn't have done it without you."

"Thank you for the popcorn and cider!" the children replied.

On the way home in the car, Angela said, "Thanks for sharing your grandparents with me. Mine live far away and I miss them. Your grandparents are a lot like mine. I had fun!"

Share with God's people who need help.
Bring strangers in need into your homes.
Romans 12:13 ICB

INCLUDE OTHERS.

If you see a need, ask friends and family to help. Share your joy.

Making Room

Sharing is sometimes more demanding than giving.

———— ■ ————

Luke's church sponsored several refugee families from Bosnia, and Luke and his family decided to share their home with a family of three. While the parents worked and took night classes to learn English, the son, Zoffi, went to school with Luke. Zoffi understood English better than his parents did, but school was still hard for him.

For the first month, Luke stuck close to Zoffi, helping him with homework, introducing him to other kids, and sharing his toys and bedroom. Wherever Luke went, Zoffi went too. Luke knew it might be a year before their Bosnian guests would be able to get a home of their own, and he began to tire of his "shadow" after several weeks. *Zoffi needs more friends than just me!* Luke thought.

Luke had also come to see that he and Zoffi had different interests. When Luke played baseball with his friends, Zoffi insisted he'd rather watch. And even though the football coach said there was room for one more on the team, Zoffi said he needed the time to study. Luke was sure that if Zoffi would play, he'd make more friends. Then one day at home, Luke heard Zoffi picking out songs on the piano and singing along. Suddenly Luke had an idea.

The next day at school, Luke took Zoffi to see Mr. Glover, the director of the school chorus. "He's got a great voice!" Luke told Mr. Glover.

"Wonderful! Welcome to the chorus, Zoffi!" the teacher said.

Zoffi not only made new friends in the chorus, but the music helped him learn English faster.

Luke said a prayer of thanks that he'd figured out how to help Zoffi make friends and fit in.

Share with God's people who are in need.
Practice hospitality.
Romans 12:13 NIV

SHARING IS A JOYFUL EXPERIENCE.

If there are new children from other nations in your school, do your best to make them feel welcome.

Get the Picture?

Honesty is the first chapter of the book of wisdom.

———— ■ ————

Roger and his best friend, Kendall, were bored. After almost two hours of video games, they wanted something new to do. It was pouring rain outside, so they were trapped in the house.

"I guess I'll just go home," Kendall finally said.

"No! Wait!" Roger pleaded. "I'll think of something." A few minutes later it came to him.

"We can take pictures and e-mail them to people!" he said. "My dad just got a new digital camera."

"Are you allowed to use it?" Joey asked.

"I'm sure he wouldn't mind," Roger said, running upstairs to get it.

Soon the two boys were snapping away. And then Roger dropped the camera on the basement's cement floor and was horrified to see a crack in the case. Then, worst of all—he couldn't get the camera to work anymore.

"I'm outta here!" Kendall exclaimed, running for the stairs.

Roger thought about hiding the camera, but he knew his dad

would find it.

"Hey, Rog!" a voice called from upstairs. It was Dad!

"Down here!" Roger answered in a quiet voice.

When his dad appeared, Roger took a deep breath and explained what he had done.

"Roger, I'm disappointed in you for borrowing my camera without permission," Dad said, "but I'm proud of you for telling the truth. Mom and I will decide what your punishment should be. Next time remember to ask before you borrow something. You can see what happens when you break the rules."

"Yeah," Roger said, "you break the camera! Don't worry, Dad. I won't do this again. From now on you can be the only family photographer."

Even a child is known by his actions,
by whether his conduct is pure and right.
Proverbs 20:11 NIV

HONESTY KEEPS YOUR CONSCIENCE CLEAR.

The best way to handle a mistake is to own up to it quickly. Ask God to help you tell the truth and ask for forgiveness.

The Visit

Nothing changes a bad situation like a good word.

———— ◼ ————

"We need to hurry," Mom said to Viona. "We want to make sure we get to see Felix before visiting hours are over."

On the elevator ride to the eighth floor of the hospital, Viona said, "Mom, I'm nervous. What should I say to Felix?"

"Felix has been your friend for years," Mom said. "Just say what you'd say to him if he wasn't sick!

"But he IS sick," Viona said. "He has cancer, and that means he might die."

The elevator stopped, and Mom and Viona walked out. "Let's sit here just a bit before we go in," Mom said as she led Viona to a waiting room with a few chairs. "Vi, nobody but God knows if he is going to die. I'm praying and believing that Felix is going to live, and before we leave tonight we're going to hold hands with Felix and ask God to heal him. Whether God heals Felix or not is God's job. Our job is to pray with faith."

Mom continued, "Our job is also to encourage Felix. We need to tell him that we love him and that we are looking forward to when he comes home. We need to tell him about things that are going on in the neighborhood, so he won't feel as if he's missing anything."

"Got it," Viona said. They got up and walked toward Felix's room.

"Hey, Felix," she said cheerfully, "we sure could have used you last night. We got clobbered on the soccer field 8 to 2. Let me tell you about the game."

Felix wanted all the details. For the next half hour he forgot he was sick.

Give our best wishes to the believers.
Colossians 4:15 TEV

A POSITIVE WORD HAS POWER.

The good words you say to another person can change that person's life—for GOOD! Ask God to show you the very best thing you can say to the next person you meet.

Doing Your Part

He who moves a mountain starts by carrying away small stones.

———— ■ ————

The Miller family—Mom, Dad, Cass, Joel, and Chrissy—went for a bike ride. It was a gorgeous day in May, and the bike path that took them past the lake gave them a great view of the water.

As the family rounded a bend, Joel noticed some plastic bags and Styrofoam cups near the edge of the path. A few yards ahead he saw paper napkins, soda bottles, and other items that didn't belong on the ground.

At the end of the ride Joel said, "Dad, who threw all that trash on the ground? It looks really bad."

"Not everyone is as responsible as you are, son," Dad said.

"We should do something about it," Joel said. "I'm just not sure what."

"Why don't we come back tomorrow with some trash bags and clean things up?" Chrissy suggested.

"That sounds good," Joel said. "With all this trash, though, it could take us a while."

Joel thought about the problem on the way home and came up with a plan he thought would work. As soon as he got home, he started calling his friends and asking them to come along the next day to help. He even convinced some of their parents to come.

Joel and his crew arrived early the next morning. Within a few hours, the bike path and the beach were beautifully trash free. After everyone had gone back home to shower and change clothes, several of the parents treated the group to ice cream.

"That was fun," Joel said, biting into his ice-cream cone.

"It always feels good to do something that makes the world a better place," his dad said.

Remember

"Here is a simple, rule-of-thumb guide for behavior:
Ask yourself what you want people to do for you,
then grab the initiative and do it for *them*."
Matthew 7:12 MSG

IF YOU DON'T DO IT, WHO WILL?

You Can Do It!

Instead of sitting around and waiting for somebody else to fix something, why don't you think of a way to make it better? It's a great way to help your neighborhood.

Plan B

Life is all getting used to what you're not used to.

———— ■ ————

Anna and Bobby were eager to be with their grandparents for Christmas.

"I hope Papa likes the planter I made for him," Anna said. It was December 23, and the Chases made a list of things to pack for the two-hour drive to their grandparents' house.

"I'm sure he will, Anna. Bobby, have you packed Grandma's gifts?" Dad asked. Bobby had decorated picture frames for their school pictures to give to Grandma. "Yes, I put everything I need in a stack. I'm ready!"

"Let's get to bed early," Mom said. As the family slept, snow began to fall. Father looked out at the window when he got up. Snow covered everything! And it was still snowing.

He turned on the radio for a weather report. There was more snow to come! He called the highway department. "How are the roads to Springfield?"

The news wasn't good.

"Children," Father said, "we have to cancel our trip to Grandma and Grandpa's. The roads are really bad all the way."

Anna and Bobby were disappointed. "Now what will we do?" Father called Granddad to tell him the news, and then he went out and shoveled off the drive. At least they could get to the Christmas Eve church service.

The electricity was off at church, but it was Christmas Eve, and everyone wanted to be there. It was cold and dark. They used candles for light, and everyone kept their jackets, sweaters, hats, scarves, and mittens on during the service.

"That was an adventure!" Anna said. Bobby nodded and added, "Just like 'olden days' huh, Dad?"

Dad laughed. "Sometimes we just have to make the most of what we can do," he said.

Remember

"I came to give life—life in all its fullness."
John 10:10 ICB

LOOK FOR A SILVER LINING IN EVERY CLOUDY SKY.

When things don't turn out the way you want, then turn it around by finding the positive things in each situation!

Where Are You Going?

If you're willing to admit you're all wrong when you are, you're all right.

Wynn was watching cartoons one hot day during summer vacation when the phone rang. It was his friend Mark, inviting him to swim at the city pool.

"You bet!" Wynn said. "I'll be right over!" He ran to his room to put on his swimming trunks and flip-flops and grabbed a beach towel from the linen closet. Looking out his bedroom window, he saw his mom in the backyard, working in her garden. He thought about yelling out to say where he was going, but he didn't want to disturb her. Besides, she knew Mark, and she'd probably guess that he was at Mark's house if she needed him for something.

When Wynn got to Mark's, Mark's older brother drove them to the pool. Soon Wynn and Mark were splashing around in the cool water and having a great time.

When Wynn got home three hours later, he was surprised to see his dad's car in the driveway. It was only two o'clock in the afternoon.

"Wynn!" his mom cried out when he walked through the door. "Where have you been?"

"At the pool, with Mark," Wynn said.

"I was scared to death!" his mom said. "I didn't know where you were."

"I'm sorry, Mom," Wynn said. "I figured you'd know I was with Mark."

"Wynn, you should never leave the house without telling Mom or me where you're going," Dad said sternly. "We always need to know where you are, to know that you're safe."

"I understand," Wynn said. "Next time I'll be sure to get permission, so you don't have to worry."

Our love for God means that we obey his commands.
And his commands are not too hard for us.
1 John 5:3 TEV

KEEP YOUR FAMILY'S RULES.

Being part of a family means obeying your parents. Telling them where you're going is an easy rule to follow. It helps keep you safe, and your safety makes them happy.

What's Most Important?

———— ◆ ————

"Eldon, how are you coming on your pledges?" Eldon's dad asked at breakfast.

"Great! So far I've got twenty-two dollars for every lap I run. I'm going for my all-time best! I think I can raise more before the deadline."

The annual fund-raiser was for a local school for disabled children. The school was important to the Carlisles since Eldon's younger sister, Julie, was a student there. She had multiple disabilities, and the family depended on the school in many ways for her education and physical therapy.

This year Eldon had asked his Sunday school class to join in. Every year his class took on a project to help others, and this year it had selected Julie's school.

Mr. Carlisle said, "Eldon, you know that Julie really wants to run this year. Your mother and I think she can do it, but you would need to run with her. What do you think?"

Eldon hadn't been counting on that. He was planning to do

his very best at running too. He thought he could win his age division. "Dad, do I have to? If I have to run with Julie, I won't have a chance at winning my division."

"I know that's a lot to give up. Think about it. You know how much Julie looks up to you."

Eldon talked it over with his friend. "What's the right thing to do? I really wanted to make this my best year."

"Julie's a great kid, El," his friend said. "You mean a lot to her. You won't win the race, but I think it's the best thing to do."

Eldon finally agreed. He and Julie ran and walked their laps together. They didn't win a ribbon for the best time...but Eldon brought in the most money!

Let us run the race that is before us and never give up.
Hebrews 12:1 ICB

WINNING ISN'T EVERYTHING.

Take a look at some of the things you want to win. What will it cost you to win them?

Say a Prayer

How shall we comfort those who weep?
By weeping with them.

Mrs. Higgins's fourth-grade science class was out of control. Some of the boys were throwing wadded-up paper at the girls, and the girls were yelling at them to stop. When the bell rang to announce the beginning of the class period, Mrs. Higgins walked into a room of chaos.

Instead of telling everyone to behave, Mrs. Higgins walked slowly to her desk and sat down. She didn't even look at her students. Ross noticed her wiping a tear from her eye.

Finally Mrs. Higgins stood up.

"Open your books to page 42," she said, and then turned to start writing on the board.

Several students continued to talk and laugh. Mrs. Higgins didn't seem to notice. Ross was puzzled. She was usually very strict. Why was she letting everybody get away with such bad behavior?

When class was over, all the students went running out of the room—except Ross, who took his time in gathering up his books.

Then he walked up to the teacher's desk.

"Is everything okay, Mrs. Higgins?" he asked.

Mrs. Higgins had tears in her eyes again. "No, it's not," she said softly.

"What's wrong?"

"My husband is in the hospital, and I don't know what's going to happen to him."

Ross hesitated, and then he decided to go for it.

"Would you … I mean, could I maybe pray for you?" he asked. "My mom and dad pray for me when I'm sad about stuff, and it really helps."

Mrs. Higgins smiled. "That would be great," she said. "I think that's just what I need to make me feel better."

Help carry one another's burdens,
and in this way you will obey the law of Christ.
Galatians 6:2 TEV

YOUR PRAYERS ARE A GIFT.

When someone you know is hurting, ask if you can pray with him or her, even if the person is older or is a leader. God is always available to listen to our prayers and comfort us when we have trouble.

Say Nothing

The reason a dog has so many friends is that he wags his tail instead of his tongue.

"Can you keep a secret?" Silas whispered.

Vic nodded his head vigorously. "Sure!"

"Edward's dad is going to lose his job!" Silas said. "My dad works at the same company. I heard him telling my mom last night. Now, remember, you promised not to tell."

"I won't," Vic vowed.

In gym class that day, Vic fouled out and watched his team lose the basketball game. Edward, who was on the winning team, came up to him and teased him about playing so badly.

"Yeah, well, maybe I let you win," Vic said, "because your dad is losing his job."

"He is not!" Edward yelled. Vic shrugged his shoulders and walked away, but he felt bad about telling the secret.

Vic's mom wanted to know why he was so quiet when he got home from school.

"I broke a promise," he said glumly. "I told Edward his dad is going to lose his job."

"You know it's wrong to break a promise," Mom said. "I think you know how much harm it can cause, don't you?"

"Yeah, because Edward was really mad."

"Did you apologize?" Mom asked.

"No. I'm too scared to."

"If you don't do it now," Mom said, "you won't be able to face him at school every day. And I think Edward could use a friend right now, don't you?"

"Yeah," Vic said. "I wasn't much of a friend to him today. I think I'll call him and see if I can go over there right now."

It is better to say nothing than to promise
something that you don't follow through on.
Ecclesiastes 5:5 NLT

KEEP YOUR PROMISES.

God wants all of us to be trustworthy. So when you give your word, make sure you keep it.

Jarrett's Joy Cart

Generosity lies less in giving much than in giving at the right moment.

—■—

Jarrett Mynear was only two years old when his family found out he had cancer. By the time he was ten, he was an expert on living in a hospital. Jarrett had lots of treatments that made him feel very bad. He also had several operations, one of them to remove part of his leg.

Jarrett had every reason to be sad. But he wasn't. One day it occurred to Jarrett that he wasn't the only kid in the children's hospital who was sick. He realized there were lots of other kids feeling as bad as he did. He decided that someone should do something to make them all feel better—and that someone was Jarrett!

He came up with a plan to fill a pushcart with stuffed animals and other toys. Kids could choose a toy to keep as the cart rolled by. With the help of his mother, Jarrett raised donations of money and toys from people and businesses in his hometown. Jarrett spent all the spare time he had setting up and running "Jarrett's Joy Cart" for the kids in the local children's hospital.

The first day Jarrett took the Joy Cart around the hospital, several local radio and television stations covered the event, and even more donations rolled in because of the news report. Even when Jarrett was feeling very sick, rolling the cart around the hospital and seeing the happiness it brought to other kids helped him feel better.

Today Jarrett's Joy Cart is giving out free toys to hospitalized children in several cities. Jarrett's family hopes others will start joy carts of their own all across the United States.

Remember

"Remain in my love.... I have told you this so that
you will be filled with my joy."
John 15:9, 11 NLT

FEEL BAD? REACH OUT TO OTHERS.

You Can Do It!

Know someone who needs a little help or just cheering up? Think of something you can do just for that person to help brighten his or her day. Small things count!

Keep Your Cool

When angry, take a lesson from technology;
always count down before blasting off.

———— ◼ ————

Cole rolled the dice and moved his game piece five spaces forward. He let out his breath in relief. He had landed on one of his own pieces of property, so there was no rent to pay.

His cousin Steven took his turn, followed by Cole's Uncle Larry. Then it was Cole's turn again. This time he wasn't so lucky. He landed on Park Place, one of Uncle Larry's properties, and it had two hotels on it. Cole grumbled as he counted out the money and saw that he only had $500 left.

Steven landed on one of Cole's properties, which helped replace some of Cole's lost cash. But four turns later, Cole landed on the "Go to jail" square.

"I quit!" Cole fumed. "This is a stupid game!" He got up and ran to his room. Uncle Larry followed him.

"Go away!" Cole said.

"Cole, I think you have a chance to learn something really important today," Uncle Larry said.

Cole was silent.

"Games are like life," his uncle continued. "Sometimes they

192

go your way and sometimes they don't. The thing to do is to decide not to get upset when you lose."

"But I hate losing!" Cole said.

"We all do," Uncle Larry said. "But if we get mad and run away when it happens, we're going to spend a lot of time being miserable. I'd rather be happy, wouldn't you?"

"I guess so," Cole said.

"Something else," his uncle said. "When you win, you want people to be happy for you, right?"

"Right."

"So when someone else wins ..."

"... I should be happy for them," Cole finished.

"Congratulations, Cole," Uncle Larry said, smiling. "You just won—big time."

Remember

A foolish person loses his temper.
But a wise person controls his anger.
Proverbs 29:11 ICB

BE A HAPPY LOSER.

Even when you lose, you can be a winner. How? By having the right attitude. Put on a smile, and see if you don't feel better.

Old Enough

Justice demands that we seek and find the stranger, the broken, the prisoner and comfort them and offer them our help.

Every Sunday Ryan stood at the door of what everybody called the "Street-Feeding Room" to watch some of the men of his church pass out sandwiches and pour coffee for several dozen homeless people who came to the church for a free meal.

"It doesn't look very hard, Dad," Ryan said to his father one day after they had dropped off a sack of groceries outside the Street-Feeding Room door.

"Oh, I think it's very hard," Dad said. "Homeless men and women are sometimes really cold at night if they don't make it to the shelter. It's hard to be hungry and not have a home and …"

"No!" Ryan said. "That's not what I mean. It doesn't look very hard to hand out sandwiches and pour coffee."

"Well, I guess not," Dad said. "What are you thinking, Ry?"

"I'd like to do that. Could I?"

"Perhaps when you get older," Dad said.

"How much older?" Ryan asked. "I'm eight."

"I don't know. Just older," Dad said.

That morning the preacher talked about a story in the Bible. A little boy gave his lunch—just a few pieces of bread and fish—to Jesus. Jesus blessed and broke the lunch, and then He passed out the food. Before the meal was over, thousands of people had eaten.

As they left the church, Dad said to Ryan, "I think you might be old enough after all to help in the Street-Feeding Room."

"Really?" Ryan said. "Can I start next Sunday? I promise I'll be really careful in pouring the coffee."

Yes," Dad said. "We'll go next Sunday morning! And, actually, I think we need to go on Saturday morning too."

"What happens then?" Ryan asked.

"That's when we make the sandwiches to hand out," Dad said.

Remember

Be kind and tender-hearted to one another.
Ephesians 4:32 TEV

ALWAYS LOOK FOR A WAY TO HELP.

Keep your eyes wide open today for ways to show kindness to any person you see who is in need of help or encouragement.

The Test

Nothing is really lost by a life of sacrifice; everything is lost by failure to obey God's call.

This was the children's first trip into the desert to watch their Dad test the horses. Five unsaddled stallions snorted and stamped as they waited. The horses could smell the water at the oasis only a little way beyond their stopping place, and they were very, very thirsty.

Leah and Logan had watched their father train the horses for months. He was able to whistle in a certain way that the horses recognized as a command to come to him. This small group of Arabian stallions did what none of the other horses in the corral had done. When Dad whistled, these five instantly came and stood directly in front of him.

So why had Dad refused to give them food or water for the past two days? And why had he brought them all the way to the desert for water at the oasis?

Suddenly Dad gave the signal to release the stallions. Desperately thirsty, they bolted for the oasis. But just as they reached the pool, Dad whistled!

Two of the horses plunged their noses into the water to take a long drink. Two others took a short drink and then turned to run back to Dad. But the fifth horse stopped the instant it heard the whistle, and, in spite of its tremendous thirst, turned and ran back until it was standing in front of the children and their father.

"This is the horse, kids! Of the five, this is the only one that we can depend on to obey its master no matter how strongly it wants to disobey. You can trust this horse with your life. The others will never be completely trustworthy."

Then their father looked deep into their eyes. "Leah and Logan, when it comes to obedience, people are not so different."

Remember

"If you love me, obey my commandments."
John 14:15 NLT

BE OBEDIENT TO GOD.

You Can Do It!

Next time your parent or teacher asks you to do something you'd rather not do, just say "Yes!" instead of "Why?"

Tough to Forgive

Forgiving those who hurt us is the key to personal peace.

Julian was upset that Lex had invited a whole group of boys to go to the ballpark with him and his dad—and had failed to invite him. "I thought we were friends!" Julian said to Uncle Jesse. "He invited eight guys to go with him, but not me. I'm the one who always helps him with his homework and covers for him when he doesn't want his dad to know where he's going or what he's up to."

"Hmm," Uncle Jesse said. "Maybe you know too much, and Lex didn't want anything to slip out of your mouth."

"Whatever ...," Julian said in disgust. "I just won't be his friend anymore."

"Hey," Uncle Jesse said. "Now's the time to be the best friend he ever had, man! Do you know what a really great friend does?"

"What?" Julian asked.

"The first thing a really great friend does is refuse to lie, cheat, or cover up. It's time Lex did his own homework and faced up to the consequences of his own choices. And there's a second thing ..."

"What's that?" Julian asked.

"A really great friend forgives."

"But Lex doesn't deserve my forgiveness," Julian said. "And he sure hasn't asked for it."

"No, but Julian, nobody deserves forgiveness—not really. And, no, he probably won't ask for forgiveness. But that's not what forgiveness is all about. Forgiveness is when you put a person who hurts you into God's hands and you say to God, 'Here, You deal with him. Please help me get over being upset.'"

"That's tough to do," Julian said.

"It is," Uncle Jesse said, "but it's the right thing. Hey—why don't we play some catch? They might be watching a game, but how about you and I play the game!"

Forgive one another,
as God has forgiven you through Christ.
Ephesians 4:32 TEV

GIVE FORGIVENESS FREELY.

One of the best gifts you can ever give to a person is forgiveness. Is there someone you need to forgive today?

Ready to Fish

Nothing can be done without hope and confidence.

———— ∎ ————

Lee looked at the boat bobbing in the water and took a gulp. Today he, Dad, and Uncle Ted were going on Lee's first deep-sea fishing trip. Lee had heard Dad and Uncle Ted tell fish stories all his life, and they always added, "We can hardly wait until you're old enough to go with us, Lee!" They hadn't seemed to notice that Lee didn't seem eager to go. In fact, Lee wasn't sure deep-sea fishing was for him.

Once, while he was in a small rowboat at the big pond in the park, the wind had blown, and the boat rocked quite a bit. Lee felt sick, the same way he felt on car trips up winding mountain roads. His dad knew that he got carsick. *Why doesn't he think I'll get seasick*, Lee thought.

Lee told Mom a few days ago he was afraid of getting seasick. Mom helped him put on a patch the doctor said would help. Lee was thankful it was in a place Uncle Ted wouldn't see it.

"God, please let this patch work," Lee said as he boarded the boat with his dad. "Please don't let me be embarrassed by getting sick."

"Hey, buddy," his uncle said as he came on board. "Sounds like it's a great day for fishing. The captain says the fish are running and the ocean is calm."

Lee stared at his uncle's arm. "What's that?" he asked, pointing to a patch.

"Oh, that keeps me from feeling seasick," his uncle said. "I always wear one just in case."

Lee smiled and felt his whole body relax. It might be a good day after all.

The devil prowls around like a roaring lion...
but resist him, firm in _your_ faith.
1 Peter 5:8–9 NASB

DON'T GIVE IN TO FEAR.

In every situation that requires courage and faith, there's somebody who is just as scared as you are. Encourage that person, and you'll feel braver too!

Planning Ahead

Good enough never is.

———— ◼ ————

Twins Benjamin and Brittany lived on a farm and raised animals to show at county fairs.

One day the twins' dad decided to give them a job they hadn't done on their own before. "Kids, I want you to mow the big alfalfa field, bale it, and get the hay in the barn before the first snow. You can work on it at your own pace, but just be sure it's done before it snows. Otherwise your animals won't have anything to eat this winter."

The twins figured the first snow should be at least a month away. The first week, they got most of the mowing done. They missed a corner here and there. *That shouldn't amount to much hay,* they thought. Week two they finished mowing and began baling the alfalfa into bales. The job took longer than either Benjamin or Brittany thought it would, so they decided to run the baler a little faster over the field. They began to miss a lot of hay, and the wire holding the hay into bales was loose.

Then school and activities began to cut their work time short, and two weeks later, when the first snow was on its way, there were still bales in the field. Dad and Uncle Charlie had to help them get it stowed in the loft of the barn.

When they finished at midnight, Dad said, "Kids, I'm afraid your 'almost good enough' job wasn't. I don't think you have as much hay as you are going to need. You'd better start thinking about how you're going to earn enough money to buy hay when that runs out this winter."

That was not what Benjamin and Brittany wanted to hear, but they knew Dad was right.

The ants are not a strong people,
But they prepare their food in the summer.
Proverbs 30:25 NASB

A JOB WORTH DOING IS WORTH

DOING WELL.

Go a little slower with that job you would rather not do; get it right the first time, so you don't have to do it over again!

Wheels

Being judgmental and condemning
is not one of the gifts of the Spirit.

———— ■ ————

Gerry had never seen the kid sitting at the desk just inside the classroom door. Students flooded into the room, but no one spoke to him. Gerry was about to say hello when Jack, his best buddy, grabbed him by the back of the collar.

"Hey, man, don't forget skateboarding at the new skateboard park this afternoon. My mom will pick us up right after school. "

"Yeah!" Gerry said. Then class began.

When the bell rang, the new kid didn't move, which was inconvenient since his chair was practically in the doorway.

"Hey, man, it's time to go," Gerry said as he roughly brushed past. But the new guy didn't move.

Just before lunch, Jack and Gerry were making more skateboard plans when they noticed Mr. Jenkins, the school counselor, pushing something down the hall. As he got closer, Gerry saw the new kid sitting in a wheelchair. Suddenly Gerry understood why the new kid had not gotten out of the way.

"Hey, Mr. Jenkins! Can I meet the new guy?" Gerry called.

"Gerry, this is Kirk." Kirk looked up.

"Cool wheels, Kirk. Lots bigger than mine," Gerry said, pulling his skateboard out of his locker to show Kirk. Both boys laughed.

"Mr. Jenkins, can I drive Kirk to the lunchroom?"

"Hey! I can drive myself!" Kirk said with a big grin as he began quickly wheeling himself away from them.

"No fair! We're not allowed to skateboard in the hall!" Gerry said, with a laugh, as he and Jack hurried after Kirk.

Help those who are weak.
Be patient with every person.
1 Thessalonians 5:14 ICB

DON'T JUDGE, UNLESS YOU KNOW THE WHOLE STORY.

Ask God to give you a patient spirit when you see someone doing something you think is disrespectful. Find out more about why he or she is doing what bothers you.

A Kind Face

Prejudices are robbers of friendships.

———— ◆ ————

"I hate them! I HATE them!!" Jeff cried. He had fought back his tears on the way to the hospital, but the sight of his dad in a hospital bed hooked up to those tubes was more than he could take. The vicious gang members had no reason to attack his father—they had mistaken him for a member of a rival gang because of a piece of clothing he wore for his job.

"Those people are evil!" Jeff cried as he plopped down on a chair in the waiting room and buried his face in his hands.

Gently an unseen arm slid around his shoulders, and a woman's soft voice asked, "What people, honey?"

"Down in the projects—gangs and people on drugs—all those people in the ghetto!"

The soft voice came again. "Honey, the ghetto is full of all kinds of people. Some of them are really bad—like the ones who hurt your dad. And some of them are good—like me."

The words didn't sink in at first, but Jeff slowly raised his head to see the kindest face he'd ever seen. She looked like his grandmother, except she was black.

"I … I'm …," Jeff was so sorry he could hardly speak.

"It's okay, honey," the kind face said. "Those bad people sent my son to heaven before his time. It's all I can do not to hate them too. I just keep remembering that Jesus loves them even though He hates what they do. And it's up to you and me to keep praying that someday they'll love Jesus back."

She gave his shoulder a little squeeze and said, "The doctor said your dad's going to be okay. Let's see if you and I can work on being okay too."

Hatred stirs up strife,
But love covers all sins.
Proverbs 10:12 NKJV

HATRED POLLUTES THE HEART.

Don't lump everyone in a certain category just because of where they live, their race, or their culture. Take time to get to know people the way God sees them—through the eyes of love.

A Clean House

If each one sweeps in front of his own door,
the whole street is clean.

———————◆———————

"Time for spring cleaning!"

When Doug and Elaine heard their mom say those words, they wanted to run and hide. Now that they were older, Mom expected them to help with more of the top-to-bottom house cleaning she liked to do twice a year.

"I don't see why we have to empty out these closets," Doug grumbled as he pulled snow boots, hockey sticks, and a pair of pink mittens from a back corner.

"Wait! Those are the mittens I lost!" Elaine exclaimed.

"Lucky you," Doug mumbled, using a dust mop to clean the closet floor.

"These windows don't even look dirty," Elaine said as she sprayed on some cleaner and wiped them briskly with paper towels. She was surprised to see dirt on the towels when she finished.

"How's it going in here?" Mom asked, coming to inspect the room.

"Our house isn't that dirty," Doug said. "You clean it all the time. Why do we have to do this?"

"Remember how we didn't clean the garage for a really long time?" Mom asked.

"Yeah, it took three days to do it, and there were spiders! Ugh!" Elaine said.

"And that box of books was ruined because we didn't know that it had been sitting in a puddle of water," Mom said. "When you keep up with the cleaning, it's easier to do, and it takes less time."

Mom said, "As soon as you finish up in here, we'll be done. We can go out for pizza."

"I'm on it!" Doug exclaimed, grabbing some furniture polish. "This dust is a goner."

Remember

If a person is lazy and doesn't repair the roof, it will begin to fall.
If he refuses to fix it, the house will leak.
Ecclesiastes 10:18 ICB

CLEANER IS BETTER—REALLY!

You might not think that housework is any fun, but you have to admit that it's great when everything is clean and orderly. It's important to keep the clutter out of your heart too.

What Benjamin Did

God doesn't give people talents that he doesn't want people to use.

———— ■ ————

"You did such a good job, Arnold! Your second piano piece was especially good. Mr. Cannon asked me if I thought you would be interested in playing for the school chorus next year," his mom said.

Arnold climbed out of the car, gathered his music off the seat, and headed into the house without saying a word.

"What's the matter, son?" his dad asked when he found him sitting at the kitchen table alone.

"It's Billy," Arnold said.

"What did he do?"

"He didn't do anything. That's the point. It doesn't seem fair, Dad. I can play the piano, I get pretty good grades, play sports ... and, well, just do all sorts of things Billy will never be able to do."

Billy, Arnold's little brother, had been born with a mental disability and went to a special school.

"Well, Arnold, you are talented," Dad said. "But so is Billy. He's just talented in different ways."

"Like how?" Arnold asked.

"Do you like Billy?" Dad asked.

"Of course! Everybody likes Billy. He's almost too nice. He's a great brother."

"And he loves you too, Arnold. One of Billy's talents is that he makes everybody he talks to feel special. He's a loving kid. And he's really, really proud of his big brother."

Arnold grinned. "Yeah, this afternoon, every time I finished playing the piano, he jumped up and said, 'That's my big brother!'"

"Billy's just as gifted as you are, Arnold. Just in different ways."

Arnold had to agree.

Remember

We all have different gifts.
Romans 12:6 ICB

TALENTS COME IN DIFFERENT SIZES AND SHAPES.

Practice the talents you have, and appreciate the talents of those around you.

Being There

A true friend is someone who is there for you when he'd rather be anywhere else.

———— ■ ————

Dad hurried into the school. He didn't like the sound of the call he had received. A woman's voice had said simply, "Mr. Jefferson, you need to come pick up your son at the principal's office."

What could Davis have done? he wondered. *He hardly ever breaks any rules at home, and he doesn't like to fight.*

As he walked up to the school office, Dad could see Davis and his friend Joey sitting on the bench just outside the principal's door. Joey was holding an ice pack up to his face, but Dad could see he had a black eye.

"What's going on?" Dad asked. His voice sounded a little stern.

"Hi, Dad," Davis said. "I'm just sitting here with Joey."

"What happened?" Dad asked. "Were you and Joey fighting?" Before Davis could say anything, Dad added, "You and Joey are friends, Davis. Why would you be fighting?"

"We weren't fighting, Dad," Davis said. "Joey's locker was open, and one of the guys—Ed, he's a bully—pushed Joey into the edge of his locker door and gave him a black eye." Pointing to the closed principal's door, Davis added, "Ed is in there with the principal and his mom right now. The principal asked Joey to wait out here."

"Well, what are you doing here?" Dad asked.

"I'm just sitting here with Joey, being his friend," Davis said. "I asked the lady to call you on your cell phone to tell you where I was because I wasn't out by the curb."

Dad sighed a huge sigh of relief. "Mind if I sit here and be a friend too?" Dad asked.

Joey looked up and said, "Sure. A guy can't have too many friends at a time like this."

Remember

Some friendships do not last,
but some friends are more loyal than brothers.
Proverbs 18:24 TEV

"JUST BEING THERE" IS OFTEN ENOUGH.

Your presence is sometimes the best present. Is there somebody who needs to have you close by his or her side today?

Sharing Your Faith

"Once you become a Christian," the Sunday school teacher said, "it's very important to tell other people. The Bible tells us to share the 'good news' with others."

Evan and Celia, who had been Christians for several months, told their family and most of their friends that they had asked Jesus to come into their hearts. There were two friends, though, who weren't interested: Jerry and his sister Ruby.

"We don't want to talk about religion stuff," Jerry had said. "Let's go play horseshoes."

Evan and Celia did not mention God to Jerry or Ruby anymore. They felt sad, though, because they really liked Jerry and Ruby and wanted to make sure they would all be in heaven together someday.

Evan decided to be brave and invite their two friends to the Sunday school picnic.

"No way—no church stuff," Jerry said.

"There'll be horseshoes," Celia said.

"Horseshoes?" Jerry perked up. "Well … maybe we could go."

The four friends went together and enjoyed all the great food and games. At the end of the day, Ruby said, "I didn't think I would like church people, but they're not so bad."

"Yeah, nobody tried to force me to get saved," Jerry laughed.

"We don't do that," Celia said. "We just tell you the truth about God and let you make up your own mind."

"I guess I can handle that," Jerry said. "Maybe I'll come check out that church of yours sometime."

"You do that," Evan said. "We like to share the things we love with our friends."

Remember

"And those who put others on the right path
to life will glow like stars forever."
Daniel 12:3 MSG

SPEAK UP ABOUT JESUS.

Sometimes it's hard to talk about Jesus with people who don't want to hear about Him. But those are the very people who need to hear about Him, so don't give up.

Friends Forever

A friend can tell you things you don't want
to tell yourself.

——— ■ ———

Calvin and Dean had been inseparable best friends since second grade. Then two years later Calvin's parents divorced. When his mother got a better job, Calvin had to move to another city. He came back to spend summers with his father.

Calvin had to take on more responsibilities, like vacuuming and helping with meals before his mother got home from work. He spent more time on his own while his mother worked.

He and Dean kept in touch by e-mail. They were both excited about being together.

Calvin called Dean's house as soon as he got to his dad's. "Hello. Is Dean home? This is Calvin."

"Good to hear you, Calvin. This is Mrs. Williams. How are you doing? Dean has sure missed you."

"I can't wait to see him. Can he spend the night tonight? My dad said it was okay."

"Sure. I'll have him call you."

Mr. Williams took Dean over to Calvin's. The two stayed up

late talking, and Calvin's father took them to the swimming pool the next day. It was fun to be together. But there was something different about Calvin. He used some bad language. Calvin's dad didn't say anything, but it made Dean uncomfortable.

"Calvin, you didn't used to say words like that."

"I know. I have some new friends. And that's how they all talk."

"Are you sure you want to be friends with them?"

"Hmm. Maybe you're right, Dean. It's been hard to make new friends. I guess that was the easy thing to do."

"Calvin, I really missed you. I'll always be your best friend. Let's pray that you'll meet other friends when you get back home."

Protect the truth that you were given.
Protect it with the help of the
Holy Spirit who lives in us.
2 Timothy 1:14 ICB

TRUE FRIENDS HELP YOU BE YOUR
BEST.

Say a positive word to a friend who is struggling to be his or her best.

Toys Are for Sharing

No act of kindness, no matter how small, is ever wasted.

———— ■ ————

"You already had your turn. It's my turn!"

"That wasn't long enough. You got to go twice."

"No, I didn't!"

"Yes, you did!"

Chris and Ginger had experienced a great week camping on the lake with their mom and dad, but it was about over. Tomorrow they would have to pack up the car and head home. Then back to school a couple of weeks after that. Wow, summer was going fast.

This year the family had borrowed Uncle Jim's Jet Ski for the week at the lake. Both Chris and Ginger had done well on it and had a lot of fun.

"Children, stop arguing. There is time for only one more ride each on the Jet Ski. But don't take long, because it will be dark soon and we need to pack up."

Just then Chris and Ginger spotted Romero. He had come to the lake with his grandparents, who owned the cabin next door.

Romero was playing by himself on the beach. His grandparents were sitting nearby in the deck chairs. Romero didn't have anyone to play with, and he didn't have a Jet Ski.

Chris and Ginger looked at each other. They felt bad that they had been so selfish.

"Hey, Romero," Ginger yelled out. "Do you want to try the Jet Ski? We have to leave tomorrow, and we only have time for one more ride each. You can take my turn."

Romero's eyes brightened, and his face broke into a grin. "Wow! Do you mean it?"

"Is that all right with you, Mr. Sansone?"

"Why, sure it is—if Romero would like to go."

"Wow! Thanks, Granddad. Thanks, Ginger. I'll be right back!"

Each one, as a good manager of God's different gifts, must use for the good of others the special gift he has received from God.
1 Peter 4:10 TEV

SHARING BRINGS JOY.

Share a favorite toy or game with someone who doesn't have one.

The Apology

A sincere apology heals the heart.

Mikaila and Ned and two of their friends were at the playground, which was right across the street from Mikaila and Ned's house. They had been playing freeze tag, and decided to sit and relax for a minute before starting a game of kickball.

Pam, one of the group's classmates, walked by with a friend.

"Let's ask them to play kickball," Ned suggested.

"No," Rachel said. "Pam's no good at kickball. She's not really any good at sports."

"Maybe her friend is," Jim said.

"She doesn't look very athletic," Rachel decided.

"And she has the wrong shoes on," Otto said.

"Yeah, and did you see what she was wearing?" Zena chimed in, giggling. "I don't want somebody who dresses like that on my team!"

What the friends didn't realize was that Pam and her friend were now standing just a few feet behind them. They had heard every word. Pam's friend started to cry.

"You are really rotten!" Pam shouted at them when they turned around to see who was crying. She then put her arm around her friend's shoulders and led her away.

"Boy, I feel really rotten," Ned sighed.

"You didn't say anything mean like we did," Otto said.

"No, but I didn't try to stop you either," Ned said.

"It's my fault," Mikaila said. "I started it."

"We're all guilty," Zena said. "My mom would be really mad at me if she knew."

"We can still do the right thing," Ned said. "Let's go apologize and ask them to play with us."

"What if they say no?" Rachel asked.

"We have to at least try to make up with them," Jim said.

"Ned's right," Mikaila said. "Let's go."

Remember

"This is what the Lord of heaven's armies, the God of Israel, says: Change your lives and do what is right!"
Jeremiah 7:3 ICB

THINK BEFORE YOU SPEAK.

It's not nice to criticize someone. Imagine how you would feel if someone did that to you. If you can't say anything nice about someone, don't say anything at all.

Out of Bounds

On my honor I will do my best to do my duty to God and my country and to obey the Scout Law; to help other people at all times; to keep myself physically strong, mentally awake, and morally straight.

—————— ◼ ——————

I can't possibly take another step, Craig thought to himself. The Scout troop had walked all day long. He was tired and about to fall into his sleeping bag when the troop leader reminded him and his crew that it was their turn to find and chop firewood for cooking supper.

Craig wasn't the only one who was tired. But he, Jared, and Carlson picked up their hatchets and walked off in search of firewood. They were so tired that they forgot to check out with any of the leaders before leaving the campsite. The firewood crew headed into the woods. It wouldn't take long to find firewood.

They kept walking and walking. It was taking longer than they thought.

Jared pointed into the woods, "Look! There's a dead tree we can chop for firewood."

Finally! After some serious chopping, they stacked the wood into piles they could carry. Then they gathered their gear to head back to camp.

"Oh no," they said together. "Where's the trail?"

"I don't see it anymore."

"We got too far off the path. Now what do we do?"

"I don't have my compass. It's in my backpack, and I was too tired to carry it," Craig realized aloud.

"Now what do we do?"

"We'd better stay right here and pray that somebody finds us soon," Jared said. "If we keep walking, we'll get more lost."

It wasn't long before they spotted their Scout leader, Mr. Evans, coming their way. "Hey, guys," he called out. "Do you need some help carrying the wood back?"

"Sure, Mr. Evans. Thanks for coming to find us. We chopped some good firewood for tonight's supper."

Lord God, you are my hope.
I have trusted you since I was young.
Psalm 71:5 ICB

KNOW YOUR LIMITS.

What situation do you have today that is too big for you to do alone? Ask God to send someone to help you.

It Takes a Team

I grumbled as a child with all the housework and practicing I had to do. ... Now, when I look back, I am grateful because hard work made me stronger and a more responsible person.

———— ◼ ————

"If we all pitch in, we can get this done in time to go to the football game this afternoon," Dad said.

It had rained the past couple of weekends, and the Thompsons hadn't been able to get the fall yard work done. Today was beautiful—crisp and clear, a perfect fall day!

Sara and Abe were Mustang fans and so excited that Dad had gotten tickets for the game. But raking the yard was hard work.

"Do you really think we can get it all done by game time, Dad?" Abe asked.

"If we all do our part and work together, it's no problem. Abe, you and Mom can start raking in the backyard. Sara, would you pick up the sticks? I'll bag the leaves."

They all set out to do their tasks. It wasn't too long before Abe said, "Is that all Sara has to pick up? That's easy. Raking is hard. That isn't fair."

"When Sara has picked up all the sticks, then she can fix snacks for us to take to the game."

"Then I'll have to do more work than Abe!" Sara said.

"Let's stop this right now. If we can all have fun at the game together, we can all work together."

"I shouldn't complain. I'll work fast, so I can pack our snacks as soon as I'm done with the raking," Abe said. "I'm sorry."

"Thanks! When we have work we don't want to do, we also need to work on our attitudes. Then we'll have a great afternoon at the game."

In all the work you are doing, work the best you can.
Colossians 3:23 ICB

WORKING WITH OTHERS IS FUN.

Who needs your help today? Whatever you have to do, do it cheerfully as though you were working for the Lord.

A Dangerous Weapon

If you think you know it all, you haven't been listening.

When Mrs. Westerman asked a question about the Civil War, Luanne eagerly waved her hand.

"Robert E. Lee!" she exclaimed.

"That's right," the teacher said. "He was the leader of the Army of Northern Virginia."

"Eventually he was named commander of all the South's armies," Luanne added, looking around at her classmates to make sure they'd noticed how smart she was.

"Boy, she's a smart aleck," mumbled Kenny to Ginny. "I can't stand her."

"She is smart," Ginny said.

"But she doesn't have to rub it in," Kenny whispered.

After class Luanne marched up to Kenny. "Do you need any help with your homework?" she asked sweetly. "I noticed that you couldn't answer that question about Abraham Lincoln."

"No, I don't need your help," Kenny growled. "I'd rather flunk."

"And you probably will," Luanne smiled, walking away.

"Is there a problem?" Mrs. Westerman asked.

"Not now that Miss Know-It-All is gone," Kenny said.

"It sounds like Luanne really taught you something today," the teacher said.

"Her? No way!" Kenny protested.

"Can you tell Kenny what he learned, Ginny?"

Ginny thought for a minute. Finally she said, "That it's great to be smart, because you get good grades, but you shouldn't brag about it all the time?"

"You should follow Luanne's good example, which is to study hard and do your best," Mrs. Westerman said.

Ginny chimed in, "Just don't use your brains as a weapon to make other people feel as if they're not as good as you are."

"Wow," Kenny said, standing up straighter. "I feel smarter already."

Remember

We must not be proud. We must not make trouble
with each other. And we must not be jealous of each other.
Galatians 5:26 ICB

DON'T ACT LIKE BIG STUFF.

If God has given you a really good brain, use it to do His work. Use it to help others. Just be sure not to get the idea that being smart means you're better than other people. Simply be grateful.

227

Friendly Faces

Make new friends, but keep the old; those are silver, these are gold.

——— ■ ———

Nick was nervous about his first day at his new school. His family had moved into the neighborhood only a couple of weeks ago. His mother took him to enroll in school and meet his new teacher. Mrs. Scott was really nice and very helpful.

But Nick wondered who would play with him on the playground. Who would he eat lunch with? Would anyone talk to him?

Lanier Elementary was only six blocks from home, so Nick walked to school. On the way he heard someone call his name, "Hey, Nick! It's me, Darren."

"Darren, what are you doing here? I didn't know you went to this school."

Nick had met Darren at a church he and his family had visited.

"I live with my dad during the school year, and he doesn't live far from here. So this is where I go to school."

Wow, this is so cool. I thought I would not know anyone, Nick thought to himself.

"Hey, thanks for saying hi. I wasn't sure about this first day stuff."

"Whose class will you be in?" Darren asked.

"Mrs. Scott's."

"She's cool. I was in her class last year."

Nick and Darren approached the school building, and Darren saw some of his other friends. "Hey, guys! Did you have a great summer? Meet Nick. He's new here, but not for long. He's really cool. Kurt, aren't you in Mrs. Scott's class this year? Would you introduce him to your friends?"

Nick was grateful for Darren's kindness. After school Darren met him outside to walk home together.

"Nick, how'd it go today?"

"Thanks to you, Darren, it went all right!"

Remember

Don't do anything from selfish ambition or from a cheap desire to boast, but be humble toward one another, always considering others better than yourselves.
Philippians 2:3 TEV

NEW FRIENDS ARE EVERYWHERE!

Introduce yourself to someone new in your class, or get to know someone you don't know very well. Have lunch together, or share a seat on the school bus. You can make a difference in someone's day.

Little Brothers!

[We] can't just take things into our own
hands because we've decided they're wrong.
We have to live by the rules, even when
those rules don't always seem right.

———————— ◼ ————————

"If you ever touch my things again, I'll pound you!" Trey threatened his younger brother, Daniel, within an inch of his life—or so it seemed to Daniel.

Daniel had ignored the big Keep Out sign on Trey's bedroom door when Trey was away for the weekend. And now Daniel was in big trouble. He had tried out one of Trey's golf clubs, and when he swung the club–crash! There went a model airplane Trey had put together. It was in pieces on the floor.

"I'm sorry, Trey. Really sorry." Daniel burst into tears when Trey came home. "I'll buy you another one and put it together for you. I promise I won't get into your things again. Honest."

Daniel really looked up to his big brother, and he felt worse about Trey being mad at him than about having to pay for a model.

"Daniel, I'm really angry. Don't you ever do this again! I mean it! That took me hours to put together—and now my work is ruined. Worse than that, I trusted you. I'm disappointed. I'm going to take you up on your offer, because you need to learn a lesson, even if it's a hard one."

Trey was still angry, but Trey loved his little brother too.

"I forgive you, Daniel. Please be careful. You broke my model airplane. But what if it had been worse—what if you had been hurt? This is only a toy, and it can be replaced. But you can't be. You're the only brother I have."

Remember

Now I am happy, but not because you were made sad.
I am happy because your sorrow made you change your hearts.
2 Corinthians 7:9 ICB

LEARN TO APOLOGIZE QUICKLY.

Forgive someone who has done something that hurt you. And say, "I'm sorry; forgive me," when you've done something wrong.

Sick with Jealousy

Jealousy is a blister on the heels of friendship.

———— ■ ————

"Have you seen that new spy movie?" Quentin asked Bailey.

"No, not yet," Bailey said.

"I have," Quentin said. "My dad took me and my brothers to see it on Saturday. Then we went out for pizza."

"Sounds like fun," Bailey said, wishing he'd been invited.

"Guess where we're going this weekend?" Quentin asked.

"Where?"

"To that new amusement park with all the rides and water slides and that scary roller coaster! I can't wait to ride that!"

"Yeah," Bailey said.

As the boys parked and locked their bikes on the rack, Bailey noticed that Quentin wasn't on his usual bike. "Like my new bike?" Quentin asked, noticing Bailey staring at it. "It was an early birthday present. Dad said it was a reward for getting an A in history."

Bailey was miserable all day, thinking about Quentin. At dinner that night he complained about the food. "Why can't we have pizza?" he whined.

"Bailey!" his mom said. "Fried chicken is your favorite."

"Nuh-uh," Bailey said. "Pizza is.

"And why can't we go see that new movie?" Bailey asked a few minutes later.

Bailey's parents looked at each other.

"What's going on?" his dad asked.

"Quentin-gets-to-go-to-movies-and-eat-pizza-and-go-to-amusement-parks-and-get-a-new-bike!" Bailey said in a rush.

"Are you jealous of Quentin?" Mom asked.

"Maybe a little," Bailey admitted.

"Does it feel good to be jealous?" Dad asked.

"No."

"Then let's pray right now and ask God to help you get rid of it," Dad said. "That way, you can enjoy this great fried chicken."

I say it is better to be content with what little you have.
Otherwise, you will always be struggling for more.
Ecclesiastes 4:6 ICB

BE THANKFUL FOR WHAT YOU HAVE.

Ask yourself this: Do I have love? A family that takes care of me? Enough to eat and enough to wear? Good friends? If the answer is yes, then you have everything you need.

A Real Winner

We must use our lives to make the world a
better place, not just to acquire things.
That is what we are put on earth for.

———— ■ ————

John and Eric shared the lead in the bikeathon. It was close competition between the two fifth graders, but they were far out in front of the other cyclists.

Then John took off with a burst of speed. "Sorry to leave you in the dust."

"It's not over yet," Eric yelled back.

"I'll be waiting at the finish line!" John yelled over his shoulder—and then he was gone.

John decided to guarantee his win by taking a shortcut. There was a fork in the bike path. The left trail went through woods, but the trail on the right was much shorter. It went down a steep hill and then connected with the river path.

Suddenly Eric heard a loud splash and an even louder cry for help. It sounded like John. He must have been going too fast to make the sharp turn before the river.

Eric took off on the river trail. When he got there, John had pulled himself out of the water, but his bike was totaled and his leg was bleeding.

Eric jumped off his bike. "John! Are you okay? You've got a bad cut!" He emptied his water bottle on John's leg to wash out the dirty river water and then tied a bandanna around it to stop the bleeding.

"Does it hurt anywhere else? Can you stand up?" Eric asked.

"I'm hurting, but I'll be all right," John replied. "Thanks for stopping. Go on and finish the race. You can still win."

"I won't leave you like this. Sit a few minutes, and we'll see how you are. Then we'll walk back together."

"But you need to finish the race, Eric."

"Don't worry. I know you'd do the same for me."

You are joined together with peace through the Spirit.
Do all you can to continue together in this way.
Let peace hold you together.
Ephesians 4:3 ICB

REAL WINNERS KNOW WHAT'S MOST IMPORTANT.

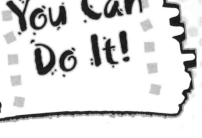

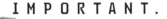

Don't let competition keep you from what's more important—helping others. Sometimes that can even mean you must sacrifice.

Birthday Giving

The covetous person lives as if the world were made altogether for him, and not he for the world.

———— ◆ ————

"Let's do something different for your birthday party this year," Mom said as she came into Preston's room and sat on the edge of his bed.

"What?" Preston asked eagerly, turning away from his computer. Mom always had great ideas for parties.

"How about asking your friends to bring a gift you can take to the homeless shelter to give to the children there."

Preston wasn't sure he liked that idea. "All my gifts would go to the homeless place?" he asked.

Mom could tell Preston was disappointed. "Preston," Mom said, "can you name for me the presents you got last year at your party?"

"Sure!" Preston said, but then he started thinking, *Was that Christmas or my birthday? Was that something I bought, or was it given to me?*

Mom pulled out a list. She said, "I know what you received." As she read through the list of ten gifts, after each one she mentioned what had happened to the gift. Four of the gifts fell into the "never played with it after the first day" category. Three were now broken. One of the gifts had been without batteries for six months. One gift was used up, and one gift Preston had given to his younger brother.

"Wouldn't it have been better to have given all ten of those gifts away to children who really would have used them?" Mom asked. "You have lots of things, Preston. And with your very generous allowance and the money you receive from family members, you can buy what you like and want to have."

"I guess you're right," Preston said.

"A birthday is just as good a time for giving as it is for receiving," Mom said.

Preston had never thought about it that way before.

Remember

Be satisfied with what you have.
Hebrews 13:5 TEV

FOCUS ON YOUR BLESSINGS.

If you concentrate on what you don't have, you can easily become greedy or miserable. Look around at all the things you do have. Start praising God for those items one by one.

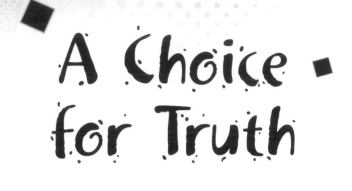

A Choice for Truth

Truth is not always popular, but it is always right.

———— ◼ ————

"It's not really a lie," Hale said. "We are going to the mall."

"Yeah," Quint replied, "but what you've got in mind is going to a movie that's in the theater at the mall."

"Right," Hale said. "But it is at the mall!"

"You know our parents haven't given us permission to see that movie. It's rated R, and our parents have told us we aren't allowed to see R-rated stuff."

"They'll never know," Hale quipped. "Everybody says this is the greatest movie they have ever seen. Don't you want to see it?"

"I guess," Quint said. "It'll be hard not to mention something from the movie if it's that great—but if we say anything about the movie, our folks will know."

"You can keep your mouth shut," Hale said.

"But will they let us in? We don't exactly look seventeen."

"Speak for yourself," Hale said. "Nobody can really tell these days if a kid is thirteen or seventeen. Act like you're seventeen, and they'll think you're seventeen."

"What if somebody asks for ID?" Quint asked.

"I've never seen anybody ask for ID, have you?" Hale asked. "Are you in or out?"

Quint thought for a minute. "I'm out."

"Out!" Hale said. "Why are you being such a nerd about this!"

"Well, I counted up the lies we'll be telling. We'll be saying we're going to the mall when we're going to a movie. We'll be acting as if we haven't seen a movie that we've really seen. We'll be saying we're seventeen when we're not. That's three lies. Three strikes and you're out. Three lies? It's not worth it to lie. I'm out."

"Well, what do you want to do?" Hale asked.

"Go to the water park," Quint replied. "I've got two free passes."

"Why didn't you say so?" Hale smiled.

Do not lie to one another, for you have put off the old self with its habits and have put on the new self.
Colossians 3:9–10 TEV

WHAT YOU DON'T SAY CAN HURT YOU.

It is easier to tell the truth than to lie, because when you tell the truth, you don't have to remember what you say.

The Car Wreck

When you have accomplished your daily task, go to sleep in peace. God is awake.

Boyd and his friend Mary Grace were sitting in the backseat of Mary Grace's mother's car, talking about things that had happened at school that day.

"It was so funny when Bart spilled that paint on his canvas in art class, and Mrs. Johnson said it looked like a great work of art!" Boyd said, remembering how everyone had laughed.

"Yeah," Mary Grace said, giggling, "and it was even funnier when Bart agreed! He said–"

CRASH! The conversation was cut short when the car smashed into another car that had run a red light at the intersection.

"Are you kids okay?" Mary Grace's mom asked anxiously, turning to look into the backseat.

Boyd and Mary Grace were pretty shaken up, but they weren't hurt.

"Don't worry," Mary Grace's mom said. "Everything will be all right."

The police came, drivers exchanged insurance information,

and Mary Grace's mom drove Boyd home. His parents were upset about the accident but grateful that their son was not hurt.

"I had my seat belt on," Boyd said. "You told me to always wear it. And it was funny, but I kind of felt peaceful the whole time."

"What do you mean?" his mom asked.

"Remember how you say that God is always watching over us," Boyd explained. "I felt like He was right there in the car. It was a neat feeling."

Boyd's dad smiled and hugged his son tightly. "It's a relief to know that when Mom and I can't be with you, God is on the job."

"He sure is," Boyd said. "He's the greatest."

He ... never tires and never sleeps.
Psalm 121:4 NLT

RELAX. GOD'S EYES ARE WIDE OPEN.

No matter how careful we are, accidents can still happen. It is so good to know that God is always with us and always knows what is happening. We don't have to worry. He's up all night! He never gets tired!

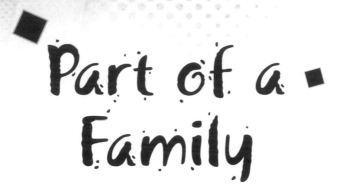

Part of a Family

The church is like a bank—the more you put into it, the more interest you have in it.

The Myers family that lived next door to Grant never missed church on Sunday. Then Mr. Myers got a big promotion and a raise at work and bought a boat. The family began to skip church to take the boat out to a lake several miles away.

Grant's dad was sad to see their neighbors spending so little time in God's house. He decided to talk to Mr. Myers about it.

When Grant's dad came home, Grant asked what had happened.

"I told him that it's important to spend time in church with other Christians," Dad said. "He said he could pray and worship God just as easily on the boat."

"What did you say?" Grant asked.

"I asked if he was doing that, and he admitted that he wasn't. He also said that he has more fun on the boat than at church."

"It does sound like more fun," Grant said.

"Grant, we don't go to church to have fun," Dad said. "We go to praise and worship God and to learn more about Him, so we can become stronger Christians."

"I think I get it," Grant said. "My Sunday school teacher said church is like a training camp."

"That's one way of looking at it," Dad said. "Church is where the Lord trains His children to take on life's problems and learn how to live together as a family."

"That can be fun, can't it, Dad?" Grant asked. "Church is serious a lot of the time, but we have fun too."

"That's right," Dad said. "God doesn't want us to be miserable. He wants us to have joy. And having joy is fun!"

"I hope Mr. Myers changes his mind about church," Grant said. "I think they're really missing out on something."

Remember

Let's see how inventive we can be in encouraging love and helping out, not avoiding worshiping together as some do but spurring each other on.
Hebrews 10:24–25 MSG

WE ALL NEED EACH OTHER.

You Can Do It!

God lives in your house, so He always knows what's going on with you. Don't you think you should go to His house and find out what He's been doing?

All Is Not Lost

If you can't change circumstances, change the way you respond to them.

———— ■ ————

Storm clouds filled the skies above the small Oklahoma town. Throughout the day loud thunderclaps caused Adrian's dog, Woofer, to whine and hide under the bed. The bolts of lightning scared Adrian a little bit too.

Adrian's parents unplugged some of the appliances and listened to weather reports on a battery-operated radio.

"Funnel clouds have been spotted fifty miles west of town and are headed this way," the reporter said. "All residents are advised to take shelter."

Adrian, his parents, his brother and sister, and Woofer went to the basement and sat down inside a large closet stocked with emergency supplies. The radio told them that the tornado was nearly there. Moments later they heard what sounded like a freight train right above their heads. The family huddled together, and Aaron could hear his dad praying.

"Everybody okay?" Dad asked when it was quiet again.

"Yes," they all said.

When they all made their way outside, they discovered a disaster. Both cars and most of the house were blown away. Adrian felt sick. His room was gone, and so was all of his stuff.

"What do we do now?" his sister asked, crying.

"We call our insurance agent," Dad said. "Then we find a place to spend the night. And tomorrow we come back and save what we can. Right now, though, we pray. We thank God for keeping us all alive. As long as we stick together and rely on God to help us, we'll be okay."

"But what about my stuff?" Adrian said.

"We all lost things we loved," Mom said, "but things can be replaced. People can't."

"It won't be easy to start over," Dad said. "But if we can survive a tornado, I think we'll be just fine."

Remember

The Lord is good to those who put their hope in him.
He is good to those who look to him for help.
Lamentations 3:25 ICB

YOU CAN ALWAYS TRUST GOD.

In your darkest moments, stop and pray. Think about how much God loves you and how strong He is. He can do anything.

Appearances Are Only That!

Thenceforth, in the nature of things, [the wolf cub] would possess an abiding distrust of appearances. He would have to learn the reality of a thing before he could put his faith in it.

Raymond and Matthais were in the same class. Raymond really admired Matthais—he got straight As all the time. He could read without missing any words. And his math papers were always perfect. Besides that, he was cool!

Raymond wished he was as smart as Matthais—then life would be perfect. Raymond wasn't all that great as a student. He hated reading out loud or having to speak in front of the class.

It was a rainy day at the end of the semester, and Raymond and Matthais stood inside waiting for the bus to come. They had their report cards. Matthais looked scared. Raymond couldn't imagine what could be wrong.

"Hey, are you all right? You don't look like you feel very good," Raymond said.

"Uh, I'll be all right … I think," Matthais replied.

"I'm not so sure," Raymond continued.

"Well, it's my grades. I made a C in geography," Matthais finally admitted.

"Wow, you always get As. I made a C—I have a hard time remembering how to spell the names of all those countries. But you're so smart. I thought As just came easy for you."

"I wish!" Matthais said. My dad doesn't let me do anything until all my homework is done. I have to study ahead into the next assignment. I have been studying. He's going to be upset, because I think I need a tutor, and I don't know if we can afford one."

"Matthais, I'm sorry. I just thought ..."

"It's okay. Everybody thinks my grades come easy. I guess because I try not to complain. I was just disappointed in my grade. See ya later," he called as he stepped onto his bus.

I guess everything isn't always the same on the inside as you see it from the outside, Raymond thought.

Remember

Thank the Lord because he is good. His love continues forever. That is what the people the Lord has saved should say.
Psalm 107:1–2 ICB

THINGS AREN'T ALWAYS WHAT THEY APPEAR TO BE.

Give thanks to the Lord for what and who He made you to be—He made you exactly according to His perfect plan.

Off Limits

Parents can only give good advice or put [their children] on the right paths, but the final forming of a person's character lies in their own hands.

Blair and Connor had worked on their project for the science fair for days. They were both good in science and hopeful of winning a prize.

"We've got some time before your dad comes to pick you up. I know some really cool Web sites on computer games," Blair suggested.

"Let's take a look," Connor agreed. "Hey, that's cool."

"Look at this one," Blair suggested. And he clicked to another Web site.

"Let's go to this one," Connor replied.

"Hey, this is strange," Blair said.

"Too strange. Let's not do this." Connor responded. He wasn't so sure he should be looking at this.

It wasn't long before Connor's dad was at the door to take him home. "How's the science project?" he asked Connor on the drive home.

"It's finished," Connor answered. He didn't have much to say the rest of the way home.

Connor went to his room after dinner. Later his dad went to say goodnight. "How are you doing, Connor?" he asked. "You've been really quiet tonight."

"I'm fine," Connor replied. "I'm tired. We worked hard."

"Is something on your mind?" he asked.

"Dad, I did something I wasn't supposed to do today."

"Do you want to tell me about it?"

Connor told his dad what happened. Connor and Blair both knew they were looking at pictures they shouldn't be seeing.

"We really do need to be extra careful about what we look at especially on the Internet."

"You're right, Dad. I'll be more careful next time. Thanks for listening."

Remember

"This is why I always try to do what I believe is right before God and men."
Acts 24:16 ICB

YOUR CONSCIENCE HELPS YOU DO RIGHT.

When temptation is near, choose to do what you know is right. Pray and ask the Lord to help you do the right thing.

What Comes First

We all find time to do what we really want to do.

━━━━ ■ ━━━━

When the new television programs came on in September, Clark felt like Christmas had come early. There were some new comedies he really liked and a show about a superhero, based on his favorite comic book.

Besides TV, Clark liked math. He regularly took part in math contests between his school and other schools. Clark's parents were proud of him. In October, though, they ran into Clark's math teacher and that he wasn't doing as well in class and might be dropped from the math team.

It was time to have a talk with Clark.

"I'm doing okay," Clark protested. "I don't know why everybody's so upset."

"You've always been able to handle a lot of activities and do well in all of them," Dad said, "but I think you're doing something now to mess that up."

"What?" Clark asked.

"You're watching too much television," Dad said.

"TV has become more important to you than anything else,"

Mom said. "Do you still read your Bible every night and pray before you go to bed like you used to?"

"No," Clark mumbled, hanging his head. "I'm too tired."

"I think it's time to figure out what's most important and focus on that," Dad said. "TV is fun to watch sometimes, but it doesn't help you with math."

"How about if we say, one hour of TV a day?" Dad suggested.

Clark wasn't too happy about it, but he understood that his parents were helping him set the right priorities in his life.

"You just learned how to give up something you think is good for something you know is better," Dad said to him. "When you can do that, it's a sign you are really growing up."

Remember

"Seek first the kingdom of God and His righteousness, and all these things shall be added to you."
Matthew 6:33 NKJV

WHAT IS MOST IMPORTANT TO YOU?

There are so many fun things to do in this world. Then there are the things we know we have to do. God can help you figure out what to do and when to do it.

The Bad Ankle

The man who understands his foolishness is wise.

———— ■ ————

Joey loved the track. Relay races and the long jump were his two best events. He couldn't wait until he was older and bigger, so he could do the high jump and the pole vault. Someday, he hoped, he would be good enough in most of these events to win world championships.

At practice on Friday, Joey and three other boys competed against four teammates in a relay race. It was a warm-up for a track meet that was scheduled for the next day.

Joey was running the third leg of the race. As he rounded the curve of the track, he stumbled and turned his ankle. He jumped up and kept running. His team came in second.

"Are you okay?" the coach asked Joey, coming to examine his ankle.

"Sure, Coach," Joey said. "I just tripped. I'm fine."

That night at home, Joey's ankle was aching. The next morning it was swollen. Joey wrapped it with an elastic bandage the way he'd been taught, put on his socks and shoes, and went into the living room.

"Ready to go?" Dad asked. Then, seeing how carefully Joey was moving, he said, "Are you hurt, son?"

"No, Dad," Joey said. "I'm fine."

"Did you hurt your ankle?" Dad probed.

"It's nothing," Joey said. He took a few steps, felt a pain, and made a face.

"You're not running today," Dad said.

"But I really want to run!" Joey wailed.

"If you ran today and got hurt worse, you could miss the rest of the season," Dad pointed out.

Joey thought for a moment. "Then I'd really be hurting the team. I guess it would be better not to run today."

"Smart decision," Dad said. "Let's go cheer on your team-mates, shall we?"

Remember

Do not be interested only in your own life,
but be interested in the lives of others.
Philippians 2:4 ICB

BE A TEAM PLAYER.

You Can Do It!

Everything you do and say affects someone else. Make sure you are doing what will be best for everyone in the long run.

The Highest Honor

For it is the enlarging of the human adventure that sports are all about.

——— ■ ———

It wasn't long before basketball season was to begin. If Collin wasn't practicing at school, he was shooting baskets at home.

Nicholas and Collin were best buddies. Collin was short but loved the game. Nicholas was the high scorer and played every game. Both Nicholas and Collin made the team.

Collin didn't get to play many games. His parents were concerned that he would want to quit. "I love being part of the team. They're the greatest!" Collin said to his parents.

When Collin did get to play, he often threw the ball to other players to go for the basket. His dad asked him why he didn't take the shots.

"Dad, there are other guys who don't get to play much either, but they can make baskets better than I can. I love basketball, but I don't always have to be the one taking the shots."

The Jaguars had a winning season. When the time came for awards at the school assembly, all the parents came, including Collin's. They didn't expect him to win anything, but they knew he wanted them to be there to support the team.

The High Score, Best Improved, Most Valuable Player awards were all passed out. Collin cheered for each of his teammates who won a trophy.

Then Coach Hubbard said there was one more award—the Sportsmanship Award. It was new this year, but the teachers voted to award it. And the first Sportsmanship Award was given to Collin Griffin!

Collin couldn't believe his ears. His classmates cheered him on. "Coll-in! Coll-in! Coll-in!" They kept it up until he got to the awards table. And then they let loose with a standing ovation.

Collin thought to himself, *This really is the greatest team in the world!*

Iron can sharpen iron. In the same way,
people can help each other.
Proverbs 27:17 ICB

A GREAT ATTITUDE WINS EVERY TIME.

If you don't get a lot of playing time—or even if you didn't make the team—you can cheer for it. Every team needs fans to help it win.

Trust with Joy

If you have no joy in your religion,

there's a leak in your Christianity somewhere.

———————— ◆ ————————

So far this week Miles had overslept, missed the school bus, forgotten his lunch, dropped his book bag in a puddle, and was caught running in the halls.

It hadn't been a good week, and it got worse on Friday, when Mr. Beyer gave a pop math quiz, and Miles got five of the ten questions wrong.

"Boy, that's really lousy," said Miles's friend Ted, looking at his paper.

"Yeah," Miles agreed. "I'm going to have to do that extra-credit assignment for sure."

As the two boys were walking to their bus after the last class of the day, another boy who was two grades ahead of them came running past. He crashed into Miles and nearly knocked him down, but kept on going.

"Hey!" Ted yelled, ready to go after the older boy.

"Let it go," Miles said. "I'm okay."

"You can't let him get away with that!" Ted protested.

"I've got to practice my lesson," Miles said calmly.

"What lesson?" Ted asked.

"My Sunday school lesson. This week we're all supposed to practice Philippians 4:4, Be full of joy in the Lord always. That means that no matter what happens, we're supposed to remember that God has everything under control, so we don't have to freak out when bad things happen."

"Like missing the bus and forgetting your lunch?" Ted asked.

"Yeah—and getting a rotten grade on a math quiz," Miles grinned. "It's hard not to get upset, but it does feel good to know that Someone is watching out for me."

Rejoice in the Lord always.
Again I will say, rejoice!
Philippians 4:4 NKJV

TRUST GOD TO GIVE YOU JOY!

In the middle of the worst day of your life—or the worst week—you can be sure that God is right in the middle of it with you, and He doesn't want you to worry. He will take care of it!

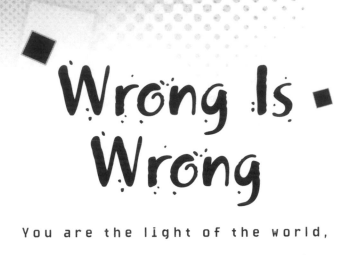

Wrong Is Wrong

You are the light of the world,
but the switch must be turned on.

Sitting in the room outside the principal's office, waiting for his dad to arrive, Trey grew more nervous by the minute.

He was in the office because he had been caught taking a dollar out of another student's desk.

"I didn't mean to do it!" he had told his teacher, but she wouldn't listen. The principal's secretary had called his dad, and now here he sat, wondering what his punishment would be.

His dad came and they went in. The principal said how disappointed he was in Trey, and Trey's dad agreed that taking away his recess for three weeks and having him write a paper titled "Why It's Wrong to Steal" would be a good punishment. Trey's dad said he would also take away his son's television and computer privileges at home for the next three weeks.

"Why did you do this?" Dad asked as he drove Trey home.

"I don't know," Trey mumbled. "I guess I just wanted to see if I could do it. I wasn't going to keep it. And it was only a dollar."

"It doesn't matter if it was one dollar or a thousand," his dad said sternly. "Stealing is stealing. Didn't you just memorize the Ten Commandments in Sunday school?"

"Yes," Trey said, hanging his head.

"And what's number eight?"

"'Thou shalt not steal.'"

"What do we do when we break one of God's laws?" Dad asked.

"We say we're sorry," Trey said.

"And?"

"And we don't do it again," Trey said. "Don't worry, Dad. I'm never going to do something this dumb again."

The person who keeps all of the laws except one is as guilty as the person who has broken all of God's laws.
James 2:10 NLT

LISTEN WHEN YOUR HEART SAYS NO.

There's no such thing as a "little" sin. In God's eyes, sin is sin. He gave us rules to follow so that we can live better lives. When we do what He tells us to do, we stay out of trouble.

Surprise! It's Fun!

Happiness is a perfume you cannot pour on others without getting a few drops on yourself.

———— ◾ ————

Michael had gone to the nursing home a couple of times with his parents to visit a neighbor, and he did not like going there. There was nobody his age to play with; nothing fun to do; and besides that, it always made him feel sad. But his music class had agreed to perform there one Sunday afternoon a month for the next three months. They were scheduled to sing hymns for the people who lived there.

A few days before he was scheduled to go to the nursing home with his class, Michael found out that his great-grandmother would be living there. She had broken her hip and would need full-time nurses to help her.

Granny was very happy to see Michael when he arrived on Sunday. The two of them were close, and Michael loved hearing the stories she told about growing up on a farm.

When they were done singing, Michael introduced his friends to his great-grandmother. Soon everyone was laughing as she described being chased by a bull and trying to learn to milk a cow.

"It's time to go!" the instructor finally said. The children groaned.

"Can we come back next week?" one child asked. "I want to hear more stories!"

As they were getting in the van, Michael told his teacher that he had enjoyed this trip to the nursing home.

"I guess it was because my grandma's there," he said.

"There are probably other people there who are nice to visit with too," his instructor said.

"I bet you're right," Michael said. "I'll ask Granny to introduce me to some people when I go back."

Remember

You should be of one mind, full of sympathy toward each other, loving one another with tender hearts and humble minds.
1 Peter 3:8 NLT

SEE OTHERS THROUGH EYES OF LOVE.

Sometimes it's hard to go visit people who are sick or in pain. But God wants us to care for each other—pray, talk, sing, laugh, and tell stories. That's what Jesus would do, and it's what we should do too.

The Joy Rule

Joy can be real only if people look upon their life as a service.

———— ◆ ————

"Why are you whistling?" Carson asked Mr. Samuels. On this particular Saturday morning Carson and several other men and boys from his church were raking leaves for a man who was sick. Carson couldn't help but notice that Mr. Samuels whistled constantly as he raked and sacked leaves.

"Didn't you ever hear that song 'Whistle While You Work'?" Mr. Samuels asked.

"Sure," Carson said, "but I never really understood that song! Why should a person whistle while he works? I whistle when I'm happy, and nothing about this yard full of leaves makes me happy! There are a ton of leaves here to rake up. No offense—but I'd rather be home watching cartoons."

"Ever hear of the joy rule?" Mr. Samuels asked.

"No," Carson said. "What is it?"

"The J stands for discovering what JESUS would do. That's J for JESUS."

"And the O?" Carson asked.

"The O stands for discovering what OTHERS need. O for others."

"And the Y?" Carson asked.

"The Y stands for discovering how YOU can link up what Jesus would do with what others need!"

Then Mr. Samuels said, "Mr. Morelli can't rake his leaves this fall. He's got a big need."

"J-O-Y—Jesus, Others, You," Carson said, getting the letters sorted out in his mind.

"Yes," Mr. Samuels said. "That's the J-O-Y rule of service. And when you really are doing service for another person because you believe Jesus wants it done, there's joy."

Then Mr. Samuels concluded, "And where there's joy, there's whistling!"

Remember

Always be joyful.
1 Thessalonians 5:16 NLT

JOY IS BEING PART OF THE SOLUTION.

Is there someone who needs your help? Lend a hand with a smile! You may not get paid, and you may not have fun, but you will receive joy in your heart and a sense of satisfaction that you have done God's work.

Green Pickle Greeting Cards

For those who are willing to make an effort, great miracles and wonderful treasures are in store.

———— ■ ————

Gym class just wasn't her thing—Brooke was always the last one chosen to be on a team. She didn't care a thing about hitting a ball or shooting a basket. It made no sense to her. She didn't even care about winning or losing. It didn't matter—they were just games.

Brooke simply had no interest in sports! Art was her favorite class. That is where she had talent–and lots of it! She knew that if there was such a thing as an art team she would be picked first, not last!

She thought, *Well, why not?* Just because it hadn't been done before didn't mean it couldn't be done. Brooke had an idea, and maybe, just maybe it could work.

Brooke's idea was to make and sell greeting cards. Her art class could provide the art. The students could make the cards however they wanted—computer art, watercolor, scrapbook art, oil painting, even button art. The possibilities were endless.

Hartley, Brooke's friend, was great in English and creative writing. She asked him to join the team. "Hartley, I've got this idea. It just has to work. I know it will!" And she explained the plan. "We need some awesome greetings. You would be great at that. Do you have someone who could help you?"

Hartley was on board immediately. "I have a friend who would be great at organizing a group to make envelopes." Then they would also need a sales team. They put their heads together and came up with a plan that included everyone!

"Let's call the project the Green Pickle Greeting Cards," Hartley said.

"Why that?" Brooke asked.

"When life hands you a green pickle, it's time to make relish!" Hartley said.

You are a chosen people.
1 Peter 2:9 ICB

INCLUDE OTHERS IN YOUR PLAN!

Do you know someone who feels left out? Invite that person in!

The Right Sport

To be upset over what you don't have is to waste what you do have.

———— ◾ ————

"Why are you frowning?" Grandpa asked Ricky.

"I'm just not any good at basketball," Ricky said. "I'm too short."

"I see," Grandpa said. "I didn't know you even liked basketball."

"I don't, really," Ricky said. "But my cousins are really good at it, and everybody seems to think I should be good at it too."

"Your cousins are taller than you are," Grandpa said. "They like basketball. That's their sport. You just have to find your sport."

"What do you mean my sport?" Ricky asked.

"Everybody is good at something, Ricky. God made us that way. He gave every person a few things that they are good at doing—some people call those things talents; some call them abilities. They are just natural things a person can do fairly easily and, with a little practice, usually fairly well. It's up to us to find the things we're good at."

"Like some people are good at spelling, and some are good in math?"

"Right," Grandpa said. "Not every athlete is good at every sport. Some people are good at baseball or golf. Some people are good at skateboarding or running. People who are good discus throwers are usually not good high jumpers. And some people are good at debate or chess.

"How do you find your sport?" Ricky asked. "I've already tried baseball and football and basketball."

"What do you like to play or do most of all?" Grandpa asked.

"I like to swim," Ricky said. "I'm a good swimmer, but I'm not very fast, so I don't know if I could make the swim team."

"Ever played water polo?" Grandpa asked.

"No, what's that?" Ricky asked.

"It just may be your sport!" Grandpa said.

You created every part of me;
you put me together in my mother's womb.
Psalm 139:13 TEV

WHEN GOD MADE YOU, HE SAID, "IT IS GOOD!"

God had a good reason for making you just the way you are. Be the very best YOU you can be!

The Pledge

Am I giving God what is right, or what is left?

Anton and his father drove home after a church service in which three missionaries told about their work overseas. The service was part of a weeklong world missions campaign sponsored by their church to raise support for nearly twenty missionaries. "I'd like to pledge something in the fund drive for the missionaries," Anton said.

"Like what?" Dad asked.

"Like a hundred dollars," Anton said.

"Wow, that's a pretty big amount of money," Dad said. "Do you have any idea where you might get fifty dollars this coming year? You'll have your allowance, of course, but money for the missionary drive is money to give after you give your tithe to the church."

Anton thought for a moment.

"I think so," he finally said. "Last year I bought two video games with money I got for Christmas and my birthday. This year I just won't buy any new video games."

"Is that a hundred dollars?" Dad asked.

"Not quite," Anton said. "But I can ask the neighbors if they have any chores they'd like for me to do. Maybe I can earn a little extra money that way."

"Is this something you really want to do, Anton?" Dad asked. "If you make a pledge, you really need to honor that pledge and follow through on it."

"I really want to," Anton said. "The missionary tonight said he trusted God for the money he needed to work in South America. I'm just going to have to trust God to give me the work, so I can earn some money to send to him."

"In that case," Dad said, "I'd like to hire you to wash the car next Saturday—beyond your usual chores. I'll pay three dollars."

"Only ninety-seven to go!" Anton said.

Remember

God ... will also supply you with all the seed you need and will make it grow and produce a rich harvest from your generosity.
2 Corinthians 9:10 TEV

GOD GROWS THE SEEDS WE PLANT.

You Can Do It!

What do you desire to give to the Lord's work today? Ask God to help you make the very best gift you can make.

The Marker

Waste no more time arguing what a good man should be. Be one.

—— ■ ——

The Thompsons were traveling to the home of relatives for a big family reunion over the Thanksgiving holiday when they stopped to get a breath of fresh air, some bottled water out of the ice chest in the trunk, and to "stretch their legs," as Dad said.

The rest stop was next to a small, old-fashioned cemetery.

"Look at the tombstones," Rosemarie said. "They are really big, and they have carvings and designs on them."

"Look at that one," Norm said. "It's got a big angel on top of it."

"It looks as if it might be the children's area of the cemetery," Mom said.

"How can you tell?" Norm asked.

"The graves are very close together," Mom said.

"Can we go see?" Rosemarie asked.

"Sure," Mom said. "I'll walk with you while Dad rearranges some things in the back of the car."

The children discovered that the gravestone with the angel was, indeed, the grave marker of a young girl who had died when she was just six years old. Norm read aloud the name of the girl and the dates of her life on the white marble base. Then Rosemarie read aloud this tribute carved into the stone:

"A child of whom her playmates said, 'It was easier to be good when she was with us.'"

There really wasn't anything more to be said. Mom and Rosemarie held hands as they walked back to the car. Even Norm was quiet.

"She may have been just a little girl," Mom said, "but she really made her life count. She had influence on people for good."

"I know she's influenced me," Rosemarie said.

Norm added a quiet, "Me too."

The Spirit produces ... goodness.
Galatians 5:22 TEV

KNOW GOD — BE GOOD.

If you want other people to feel good about you, think good thoughts toward you, say good things about you, and do good to you—be good!

Follow Through

———— ■ ————

"How's your missionary pledge coming?" Dad asked Anton a few months after Anton pledged to the church's missionary campaign.

"All right," Anton said, but he knew that Dad would be able to tell by the tone of his voice that he didn't really mean what he was saying. "Actually, not that great," Anton admitted.

"You had a good plan," Dad said. "What went wrong?"

"Well, I didn't get as much money for my birthday as I thought I would. And then I spent some of it ... on a video game I said I wasn't going to buy."

"So what are you going to do?" Dad asked. "Have you talked to the neighbors about extra chores you might do?"

"Two of them," Anton said. "They didn't have anything for me to do."

"Hmm," Dad said. "Sounds like you need a new plan."

"Do you think the missionaries really need a hundred dollars from me?" Anton asked.

Dad could see where he was going with that. "Anton, you

told me that you were going to trust God to help you earn the money to complete your pledge. It's one thing to do everything you believe God tells you to do and then fall short. But it's another thing to fail to ask God for help or to fail to do what God tells you to do and fall short."

Anton thought for a few minutes. "I know you're right, Dad. It's just harder than I thought. The first twenty dollars was really easy to earn and give. I just stalled out after that."

About an hour later Dad saw Anton heading for the backdoor with his hat on. "Where are you going?" Dad asked. Anton replied as he opened the door, "Out to see if I can rake some leaves for Mr. Phillips!"

On with it, then, and finish the job! Be as eager to finish it as you were to plan it, and do it with what you now have.
2 Corinthians 8:11 TEV

KEEP WORKING THE PLAN.

If God gives you a goal, trust Him also to give you a plan for reaching that goal and to give you the courage and diligence to "work the plan" until you succeed.

Keep Skating!

A handful of patience is worth more than a bushel of brains.

———— ◆ ————

Ava's brother Eddie helped her put on her elbow guards, kneepads, and helmet. Ava thought all this safety gear wasn't really necessary, but her parents insisted that she wear it if she intended to do any in-line skating.

Once the skates were on, Ava stood in the driveway and held onto Eddie for balance. He helped her to the sidewalk, pulled her hand off his arm, gave her a little push, and said, "Go for it!"

Ava rolled a few feet. This wasn't so bad! The breeze sure felt good. She was sure that in no time at all, she'd get the hang of this, and she could go skating with her friends. Then—BAM! Ava suddenly found herself sitting on the sidewalk. *Maybe all this safety gear was a good idea after all,* she thought.

Then she heard Eddie laughing. "Get up and go again!" he said.

With Eddie's help, Ava got up two more times. After her third fall she was in tears. In-line skating was no fun if you kept falling. She'd never be any good at this. "I give up!" she sobbed, pulling off her skates.

"You can't give up," Eddie said, sitting down beside her. "Did you notice that each time, you skated a little farther? You just have to be patient. It takes time to learn this stuff."

"You really think I can?" Ava asked, eyeing her brother with a little suspicion.

"Hey, if I can do it, you can too," Eddie said. "Like I said—be patient. You'll be skating circles around me in no time."

You need to be patient, in order to do the will of God and receive what he promises.
Hebrews 10:36 TEV

TAKE YOUR TIME AND KEEP TRYING.

Sometimes it takes a while to learn how to do something. Don't quit. Work hard and ask God to help you. He's a great teacher.

Make Time for Everyone

———— ■ ————

"Let's go," said Jason and Mandy. "We're ready for the water park." The two had their swimming suits on and were ready to go.

"There is only one rule," Dad said. "We have to stay together. If someone gets lost, then we'll meet back at the ticket gate."

The park was full of sunbathers and swimmers who were trying to keep cool in the hot weather. The park was packed and the lines were long.

Jason knew they had to take turns, but he wanted to go on his ride first. "Let's go first to the Pirate Ship," he insisted.

"Okay," Mandy agreed, "but then to the Mermaid Cruise!"

There were probably sixty people in line ahead of them at the Pirate Ship. *It's a good thing we came here first,* Jason thought to himself. After a long wait they boarded the ride.

"That was awesome! Let's ride again!"

"No way," Mandy sulked. "You said it would be my turn next."

"Okay, okay. But we're coming back here after that." And

they took off to the Mermaid Cruise. Afterward Mom wanted to ride the pontoon boats, and then Dad wanted to go down the Log Run.

They each had their turn at their first choice of rides. But because of the long lines, four rides were all they had time for.

"Do we have to go home now? I wanted to go to the Pirate Ship again!" Jason pleaded.

"We have to start our drive home now. We had a great day. We all kept cool and enjoyed the rides. There will be more to explore when we come back again! There was just more fun than we could take in, in one day."

"I came to give life—life in all its fullness."
John 10:10 ICB

FOCUS ON OTHERS AND YOUR WORLD GROWS.

Learn something new by doing what someone else wants to do.

Campaign Strategy

Let all you tell be truth.

◼

Darla didn't like what she was hearing from her "campaign committee"—her three friends Kent, Mindy, and H. R.

"She's spreading lies about you, Dar," Kent said.

"Like what?" Darla asked.

"Like saying you copy your English papers off the Internet," Kent said.

"And saying that you and your family are part of a radical group that keeps a big stash of guns in your basement," H. R. added

"I like the rumor about you and Matt making out in the school parking lot during a football game," Mindy laughed.

"People who know me know these things aren't true!" Darla said.

"That's the point," Kent said. "Not all the kids know you, and those who don't know you don't realize that what Priscilla is saying about you isn't true. We've got to fight fire with fire."

"What do you think I should do?" Darla asked.

"We could start telling people that Priscilla is bulimic," Mindy said. "She is really thin."

"Great!" Kent said. "And we could say she's probably moving next year, so she won't be around to be a student body officer any-way—her dad does work for a company where lots of people are being laid off."

"No," Darla said. "I'm not going to fight fire with fire. I'm going to fight fire with water—the truth. I'm going to ask her during the debate if she had anything to do with the lies being told about me and see what she says. Even if she says she had nothing to do with the lies, I'm going to say, 'I'm so glad to hear that, because you know these things about me aren't true. One of the most important things about being school treasurer is being honest.' I'm not going to lie to win. I'm going to tell the truth and win!"

Remember

If you want to enjoy life and wish to
see good times, you must keep from speaking evil
and stop telling lies.
1 Peter 3:10 TEV

THE TRUTH ALWAYS COMES OUT.

No matter what lies people may tell about you, God knows the truth, and in His timing, He will cause other people to know the truth too.

Ready for Prime Time

A winner is someone who recognizes his God-given talents, works his tail off to develop them into skills and uses these skills to accomplish his goals.

———— ◼ ————

"Let's enter the family Christmas program this year," Bretta said. "I'll play flute, Mom can play piano, and Dad can play his guitar. We have plenty of time to practice."

"What can I do?" Mark asked. "I want to play the piano."

"We'll think of something, Mark. You can be Santa's helper," Bretta suggested. Last spring Bretta had won a district award for flute performance. But with only two months of piano lessons, Mark wasn't ready for center stage.

"I don't want to be Santa's helper. If I can't play the piano, I'm not going to be in it."

Weeks passed quickly, and it was only two weeks until the family Christmas program. Mark did practice hard, but he wasn't ready. He was just learning to play with both hands. Mark sang the words to the music as he played.

Bretta was studying upstairs in her room. She started to close the bedroom door to separate her from Mark's practicing when she heard someone singing. She went to the stairs to see who it was and realized it was Mark! She had never heard him sing before. She sat down at the top of the stairs to listen.

At dinner Dad asked, "Well, are we ready for opening night? How's it going, Bretta?"

"Well, I do have an announcement to make."

Mark repeated his demand, "I'm not going to be in it if I can't play the piano."

"Here is the final cast: Dad will play the guitar. Mother will play the piano. I will play the flute. And Mark ... will have the lead as the solo vocalist!" Bretta announced. "Mark, will you do it? I heard you singing—you're great!"

"Well, sure! I didn't think I was good enough to sing. Thanks, Bretta!"

Each one has a special gift from God.
1 Corinthians 7:7 TEV

WE ALL HAVE GOD-GIVEN TALENT.

Encourage people you know to use a talent they may not realize they have.

Every Day

It is better to be faithful than famous.

———■———

"Well, how was it this year?" Dad asked Brock and Fran that evening, after they both had time to unpack and take hot baths. Brock and Fran had been at youth camp for a week, and when Dad picked them up at the church, they had seemed happy and tan but also hungry and tired. He figured that time for a talk would come after supper and before bedtime.

"It was great," Fran exclaimed. "I really liked the speaker this year. We had some good talks in our discussion groups too. Swimming in the pond and riding the inner tubes down the canal—those things are always fun."

"What did you like best?" Dad asked Brock.

"I really liked the guys in my cabin this year. And we had a really neat counselor. His name was Luke, and he was a real Christian."

Dad said, "I'm a little curious to know why you called him a 'real' Christian."

"Well," Brock said, "he made us spend time after lunch out in the woods with our Bibles, just reading whatever we wanted to read—he called it a 'quiet time.' And after the lights were out at night, he led us all in the Lord's Prayer."

"Those are very good Christian things to do," Dad agreed. "I would hope your counselor at a Christian camp would do those things."

"But Dad," Brock said, "we didn't just do those things once or twice. We did them every day."

"There's a lot to be said for faithfulness," Dad said. "It really is what makes us 'real' Christians to those who don't know Jesus as their Savior."

The Spirit produces ... faithfulness.
Galatians 5:22 TEV

FOLLOW THE LORD DAILY.

Get in the habit of doing things God's way. The best habits become your best character traits.

The Gift

Being grown up is something you decide
inside yourself.

— ◼ —

Taylor hated being the youngest in the family. He felt that he could never do anything as well as his older siblings, Tripp and Tracey. There weren't a lot of years between them, but enough that he always felt like the "little kid." *That's my place in life forever and ever,* he thought.

It was almost Christmas, and Tripp and Tracey were hinting at what they might give to Taylor. If he had guessed right, it was awesome—they were going to let him go skiing with them and their friends when they went to Gram and Gramp's condo in Colorado. He could hardly believe it! He had gone skiing with the whole family, but not with Tripp and Tracey and their friends.

Taylor was filled with anticipation. He took an inventory of his ski equipment. Everything was repaired and in good shape.

The week before Christmas Tripp and Tracey said they needed to talk to him. "Taylor," they began, "we've been thinking. You might be too young to go with our friends—maybe next year would be better."

Taylor was crushed, but he didn't argue. It was their trip and their friends. On Christmas morning there was a wrapped box with Taylor's name from Tracey and Tripp. This was no doubt the consolation prize. Even so, he opened it eagerly. Inside was an envelope with his name on it. He took out the card. It was an invitation from Tripp and Tracey—an invitation to go on the ski trip!

"Wow!" Taylor said. "Thanks! I thought you changed your minds."

"Well, we decided to give you a test to see if you were mature enough to go. And you passed with flying colors!"

[Jesus] began to grow up. He became stronger and wiser, and God's blessings were with him.
Luke 2:40 ICB

GROW UP ON THE INSIDE.

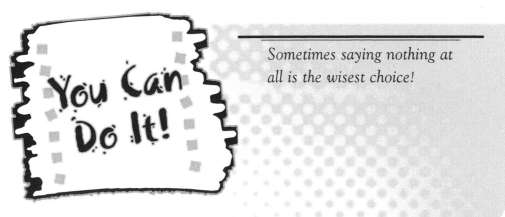

Sometimes saying nothing at all is the wisest choice!

Before You Leap...

Friends gotta trust each other ... 'cause ain't nothin' like a true friend.

———— ■ ————

"Students, we only have this hour to complete our project. Hurry and get your coats and jackets. We'll meet at the front door. We can't leave until everyone is together."

Grayson unlocked his locker and reached inside to get his jacket. Surprise—he couldn't find it. *Where is it?* he wondered. Grayson shuffled through the things lying in the bottom of his locker, and he reached up to the top shelf. He didn't have time to keep looking, because Miss Ogilvie was ready to leave. He'd have to go outside without one for now. Maybe someone turned it in at the office.

Grayson noticed that Jimmy had on the very same jacket—an NFL jacket. He and Jimmy were about the same size. Grayson wondered if Jimmy was actually wearing his jacket. He moved closer to take a look. Jimmy and Grayson had shared lockers last year. Maybe Jimmy remembered the combination and took his jacket.

"Jimmy, nice jacket you've got there. When did you get it?"

"I just got it. Perfect fit and everything. I've wanted one for a long time. Don't you have one like it?"

Grayson didn't think Jimmy's family could afford a jacket like that—they were expensive. Now what should he do? He felt sure now that Jimmy was wearing his jacket. He felt like asking his friend to give back his jacket.

Just then Grayson saw his mother drive up. She got out of the car and was walking toward him. "Grayson, you left your jacket at home this morning. It's turning colder, and I thought you might need it before the end of the day."

Thank goodness! Jimmy thought. *I nearly accused my friend of taking my jacket.* "Wow, thanks, Mom! I really do need it today," he said.

Don't testify against your neighbor for no good reason.
Don't say things that are false.
Proverbs 24:28 ICB

LOOK BEFORE YOU LEAP!

Always believe the best about someone. Investigate all the facts before you draw conclusions.

Walking Softly

Nothing sets a person so much out of the
devil's reach as humility.

"Gordon's a wimp," Jill said.

"Why do you say that?" Dad asked. "Because he doesn't play football, talk tough, or swagger around as if he's the greatest kid who ever lived?"

"No," Jill said. "He's a wimp because he backs off and never defends himself when other boys tease him. He needs to stand up for himself."

"What do they tease him about?" Dad asked.

"Oh, just stuff," Jill said. "They tease him because he walks away if they're telling dirty jokes. They tease him if he lets somebody break into line ahead of him without telling them to go to the back. Stuff like that."

Maybe I should talk to him, Dad thought. He's in the Scout troop I help to lead. I've never noticed that he backs away from any of the things we do on hikes or overnight campouts. He seems to have plenty of courage, and he always seems to be very helpful to the new Scouts in the troop.

"Gordon," Mr. White said the next time they hiked together,

"guys always seem to call other guys names. What do you do if guys call you names?"

"I don't do anything," Gordon said. "What's the point? I figure if I'm mean to the guys who call me names it sorta cancels out my being nice to other people. You can't be mean and nice at the same time."

Then he added, "My dad once told me about a president of the United States who said to walk softly and carry a big stick. Dad said he liked the saying 'Walk softly and believe in a big God.' I like that too."

Gordon's not a wimp, Mr. White thought. *He's just humble. And what a good thing that is! I need to teach Jill the difference.*

The Spirit produces ... humility.
Galatians 5:22–23 TEV

HUMILITY CAN SPEAK FOR YOU.

Many people say we have to fight our own battles, but God's Word says the Lord will fight for us. Trust God today to do all your fighting.

The Buddy System

I wish Pooh were here. It's so much more friendly with two.

——— ■ ———

Larry, Jameson, and Trevor had become best friends. They did everything together at camp: swimming, mountain climbing, hiking, horseback riding, kayaking. Soon camp would be over, and they would go their separate ways.

They planned an adventure of their own for this last day of camp. While the rest of the campers were on the scavenger hunt, they took off to swim in the mountain lake. They pulled on their swimming trunks and rolled their clothes up in their backpacks and hid them near a bush. Then they jumped into the frigid mountain water for a great swim.

How long would it be before they were missed? After twenty-five minutes they reluctantly agreed to swim back to shore. Larry went over to the bushes where they had left their clothes, "Uh, Jameson, Trevor, isn't this where we left our clothes?"

"Sure. Maybe it was another bush. Let's keep looking." Frantic searching didn't turn up their clothing.

Now what to do? They had to get back to the group. They

might as well confess their misdoings, get back with the other campers, and take their penalty.

The three walked back through the woods and out to the clearing where the other campers had gathered with their scavenger finds.

"Hey, guys, you came back with nothing—you were supposed to come back with your scavenger finds! You lose!"

"Are you missing anything? Seems our scavenger team found something no one else did—like your clothes and backpacks. What will you give us for these?"

"Next time tell us where you are going," the camp counselor said as the boys scrambled for their clothes. "In the buddy system, sometimes the 'buddy' is the group."

Remember

If one person falls, the other can help him up.
But it is bad for the person who is alone when he falls.
No one is there to help him.
Ecclesiastes 4:10 ICB

SOLVE PROBLEMS WITH COMMUNICATION.

Check in before you check out. Always tell someone where you're going to be and when!

Music to God's Ears

Praise is music to God's ears.

———— ∎ ————

"I really love music," Shanika said as she bounced her head to the music from her headset.

"Me too!" Dad shouted, hoping Shanika would be able to hear him.

"What?" Shanika asked, taking off the headset.

"Me too," Dad repeated.

"Me three," Jordie, Shanika's younger brother, called as he scurried into the room.

"Do you know where music came from?" Dad asked.

"No," Shanika said.

"Well, there's one old Jewish legend that says after God created the world, He called in the angels and asked them what they thought of His work. One of the angels said, 'There's something missing—there's no sound of praise to You.' So God made music. It was heard in the whisper of the wind and in the song of the birds. Adam and Eve learned to sing by copying the wind in the trees and the songs of the birds. Then one day they began to wonder if they had music of their own inside their hearts—after all, if every kind of bird had a different type of music, maybe they had a type of music in them. So they opened their mouths and began to sing."

"Cool," Jordie said.

"And then," Dad said, "the Bible says that way back in the time of Adam and Eve, someone named Jubal was called the 'ancestor of all musicians who play the harp and the flute.' So musical instruments were invented to go along with songs."

Then Dad gave them a challenge: "On this rainy afternoon when you can't go outside, do you think you two might be creative enough to make up a new instrument out of stuff around the house and use it to go with a new song you create?"

It took Shanika and Jordie all afternoon to discover they could!

Sing hymns of praise to the LORD;
play music on the harp to our God.
Psalm 147:7 TEV

GOD LOVES TO HEAR US PRAISE HIM!

You can make up a new song to sing to God. He'd love to hear it!

All-Out Effort

It's fun to set goals, reach goals, and reset them.

———— ◼ ————

Jett and his best buds Ernie and J. T. wanted to make the swim team. Tryouts had been held last week, and the final team members were to be announced this afternoon at the all-school rally. The friends sat together—they were excited. They felt sure they would all make it.

The principal made announcements, and then came the time for the coaches to announce who they had chosen for the swim, track and field, and softball teams. The swim coach, Mr. Carter, got up to announce the boys' and girls' swim team members. First the girls: Abby, Madison, Hope, Kayla, LaTisha, Danielle, and Carla. Now the guys' team: Miguel, Doug, Ernie, Drew, Brad, J. T., and Colin.

"Jett, what happened? There must be a mistake. Surely you made the team!"

Jett looked down, "I don't know what happened. I thought I would make it too."

The rally dismissed, and Jett and his friends headed to their next class. Coach Carter walked up to Jett. "Jett, I'm sorry you didn't make the team this year. I don't think you gave it your best effort—you weren't on time to practices, and you didn't turn in your workout reports. Everyone has to give 100 percent to be on the team. You know that."

"I'm sorry. I didn't give it my best effort. I thought I could get by without it. I let you down."

"Jett, you also let yourself down. If you really want something, you have to give it your best. You have a lot of potential for being a great swimmer. Keep working on it."

"Thanks, Coach. I'll work harder."

I do not mean that I am already as God wants me to be. I have not yet reached that goal. But I continue trying to reach it and to make it mine.
Philippians 3:12 ICB

GIVE EVERYTHING YOUR ALL.

Write down your goals and dreams. Then write down what you think it will take to achieve them. Do you have the commitment to make them happen?

Not So Cool After All

Drugs take you further than you want to go, keep you there longer than you want to stay, and cost you more than you can ever pay.

"Hey, Charles, how's it going?"

"Pretty good, Milt. Just a couple of weeks until spring break."

"I'm looking forward to that too."

"What's happening?"

"I'm meeting some guys after school. Why don't you skip ball practice and come with us?"

"I don't know about that."

"We're just going to hang around. Come after practice if you want to. We'll be at Owen's house."

"Aren't his parents out of town?"

"Yeah, but it's okay. His Uncle Jim is staying with him."

" Well, I'll think about that. I'm supposed to go home after practice."

"Just drop by on your way home if you want to. It's not far from where you live, is it?"

"Right. Okay, Milt, I'll think about it. I might see you then."

Milt was a great guy and always a lot of fun. They'd had some great times together. He didn't want to miss out, but he wasn't sure he should "drop by" without telling his parents.

Anyway, he'd think about it later. He was allowed two misses from practice, and he hadn't had any so far this year.

After practice Charles decided to head straight on home. He had a big science test in the morning, and he needed to study.

The next morning at school, the word was out. "Hey, Charles, did you hear? Milt and Owen and some other guys were busted for drugs last night at Owen's house."

"Really! Where are they now?"

"They were taken to juvenile court. Owen's parents were called home. The guys are in big-time trouble."

Charles thought to himself, *It could have been me too.*

Remember

"Change your hearts. Stop all your sinning.
Then sin will not bring your ruin."
Ezekiel 18:30 ICB

PLAY BY THE RULES.

You Can Do It!

Temptations come every day. Find out all the facts before you commit to a plan of action.

Class Hero

I had a series of childhood illnesses. The first was scarlet fever. Then I had pneumonia. Polio followed. I walked with braces until I was at least nine years old. My life wasn't like the average person who grew up and decided to enter the world of sports.

———— ■ ————

Justin was diagnosed with leukemia in second grade. He experienced a rough year of chemo treatments that left him with a bald head and his face and body swollen from strong medicine.

His fourth-grade class "adopted" Justin and the Banales family—if there was anything they needed, the class was there to help. When the family needed to go to a children's hospital in another state for tests and treatments, fund-raisers helped with expenses. When Justin's mother needed to stay with him in the hospital, the mothers club volunteers helped care for Justin's sisters. When Justin needed nursing care at home, volunteers signed up for four-hour time slots. The Banales family believed in prayer, and they prayed often for Justin's healing.

Now, two years later, it seemed that Justin had won the battle. The family was off to a cancer hospital for tests. The Banales had reason to expect good results.

Miss Catalano, the fourth-grade teacher, arranged ahead of time to have Mrs. Banales call the class at school when the reports were in. She had her cell phone with her when the call came. Her phone rang in the middle of geography class, and she answered it. "Justin, this is your mother. She has something to tell you."

Justin looked puzzled—this was unusual. He wondered what was up.

"Hello," he answered.

There was a silence.

"Really? Do you really mean it? Wow! Thanks, Mom, for calling!"

"What's the news, Justin?"

"I'm cancer free!"

The fourth-grade class stood and cheered for Justin. He was more than a survivor to them. He was their hero.

Remember

If one part of the body suffers, all the other parts
suffer with it; if one part is praised,
all the other parts share its happiness.
1 Corinthians 12:26 TEV

WE NEED EACH OTHER.

Find a way to help someone in need today. You can't do it all by yourself. But you can rally a group together in support of the person!

Every Little Bit Counts

As the purse is emptied, the heart is filled.

Gideon stared at the quarter in his hand. *My offering is so little*, he thought, *it won't make any difference if I put it in the offering plate at church. Nobody would miss it.*

He stuck the quarter in his pocket, picked up his Bible, and went to Sunday school. The lesson that week was about a widow who went to the Temple in Jerusalem and gave an offering—two little copper coins worth about a penny. Jesus had said her giving mattered! Gideon gulped. *Maybe God heard my thoughts!* His teacher then told this story:

"There once was a prince in India who dreamed one evening that he owned a beautiful garden. The lake in it was different from any other lake in the world because it was filled with perfume. Its wonderful aroma filled the entire garden and the nearby town. When the prince awoke, he decided to make his dream come true. Although he was very wealthy, he didn't have enough money to fill a lake with perfume. So he invited every person in the country to come to a party. Each person was asked to bring a small vial of perfume and empty it into the lake.

"People from all over the nation came to the party, and one by one they poured their vial into the lake. To everyone's surprise, however, the lake didn't smell any different. The prince finally asked someone to take a sample of water near the spot where the people were emptying their vials. To the prince's dismay, he discovered the water to be just water! He realized that everyone thought their little bit wouldn't matter and had poured water into the lake instead of perfume."

The teacher said, "Nobody thought his or her little vial of perfume would make a difference. Many people feel that way about their offerings. The truth is—every little bit counts."

Gideon could hardly wait to put his quarter in the plate!

You should each give, then, as you have decided, not with regret or out of a sense of duty; for God loves the one who gives gladly.
2 Corinthians 9:7 TEV

GIVE WITH A JOYFUL HEART.

Give with joy, and God will give back to you, so you can receive with joy.

"See You Later, Grandpa."

Death is no more than passing from one room into another. But there's a difference for me, you know. Because in that other room I shall be able to see.

———— ■ ————

Grandfather was ill, and Jamie was told that he might not make it through surgery. He went to the hospital with Mom and Dad to visit Grandpa.

"Hey, Grandpa, we prayed for you in Sunday school. How are you doing?"

"I'll start feeling better when this is over."

"We prayed that you would."

"Jamie, aren't you glad for all the good times we've had? Remember that time we snagged the big turtle when we went fishing? That was something, wasn't it?"

They had done a lot together. Grandpa went to all his sports games, but he was even happier with Jamie's good report cards. They attended the same church.

"Don't forget what you learned in Sunday school and church, Jamie. That's very important. I don't know what I would have done if I hadn't had the Lord to turn to when your grandmother passed away. It makes all the difference."

At that moment the nurse came in to take Grandpa's blood pressure and listen to his heart.

"We'd better go now," Dad said.

"I love you, Grandpa."

"I love you too, Jamie."

"Bye. I'll see you later."

Jamie went to school the next morning, and his mom and dad went to the hospital to be with Grandfather. Later that afternoon Jamie was called to the office. When he got there, his father was there.

"Your grandfather passed away," Jamie heard his dad saying. "Let's get your things and go home. We're all going to miss him. But someday we will all be together again. That's part of what it means to trust the Lord."

Remember

Even if I walk through a very dark valley,
I will not be afraid because you are with me.
Psalm 23:4 ICB

GOD HELPS YOU WHEN YOU HURT.

Comfort others who have lost a family member or loved one. Write a note or make a call to let them know you care.

Psalm Singers

Every Christian sings a slightly different song, but they will all make up a wonderful symphony in the throne room of heaven.

———◼———

"Do you know what the word *psalm* means?" Mr. Thomas asked the Sunday school class. Nobody seemed to know.

"It means song," Mr. Thomas said.

"All these are songs?" Marcus asked.

"Where's the music to go with them?" R. B. added.

Mr. Thomas said, "Some people who study the Bible think they know a few of the tunes the psalm writers might have used. The people in Bible times learned tunes by listening to them and memorizing them. They didn't write down their music. But we do have a big clue about these songs. Isaac, read verse three of Psalm 40 to us."

Isaac read, "He taught me to sing a new song, a song of praise to our God" (TEV).

"I think that could mean that God can give each of us a new tune to go with the words in a psalm. Every one of you boys could come up with a different tune to the same verse. What do you say we give it a try?"

All the boys in the Sunday school class were eager to try what Mr. Thomas had suggested. They chose Psalm 40:5 as the verse they would use: "You have done many things for us, O LORD our God; there is no one like you!"(TEV). Mr. Thomas said, "You can use these words or words that mean the same thing. Put them to music by next Sunday."

"But what if you can't sing?" Les asked.

"Everybody can sing something!" Marcus said.

"And if you can't sing, you can rap!" Isaac said.

The next Sunday the boys came with their songs—five very different songs for the same verse.

"We could do this all summer!" R. B. said.

"And then give a concert at the church picnic," Les added. And so they did.

Remember

It is good to sing praise to our God;
it is pleasant and right to praise him.
Psalm 147:1 TEV

GOD ENJOYS YOUR PRAISE!

You don't have to wait for a praise and worship service to praise God. You can praise Him right now with a song you make up!

Café Rules

You can never go wrong when you choose to
obey Christ.

The Jacobs family was taking a summer road trip through four states in the southwestern part of the United States. They stopped to have lunch one day at a café just outside a small town in Texas. While they were eating, Ember spotted a sign on the café wall. "Look, Dad," she said, "they have rules in this café."

Dad looked and began to smile. "Do you children recognize those rules?" he asked. Gene looked long and hard at them and finally said, "They kinda sound familiar." Mom smiled and said, "Dad, why don't you read them aloud to us?"

Dad read:

Top Ten Rules of This Café

Rule number one: Just one God.

Rule number two: Honor yer Ma & Pa.

Rule number three: No telling tales or gossipin'.

Rule number four: Git yourself to Sunday meeting.

"I know, I know," Ember said. "Those are the Ten Commandments!"

"Right!" Dad said, "And here are the last six." He read:

Rule number five: Put nothin' before God.

Rule number six: No foolin' around with another fellow's gal.

Rule number seven: No killin'.

Rule number eight: Watch yer mouth.

Rule number nine: Don't take what ain't yers.

Rule number ten: Don't be hankerin' for yer buddy's stuff.

"That's cool," Brett said when Dad had finished.

"People across our nation know what makes for a good and decent society," Mom said. "God's commandments are not just for people in Bible times. They're for everybody all the time."

What matters is to obey God's commandments.
1 Corinthians 7:19 TEV

GOD'S COMMANDMENTS ARE FOR OUR GOOD.

God did not give us the Ten Commandments to take away our fun. No! He gave them to us, so we could have the best possible life—now and forever.

Not Like Them

We can be right without being self-righteous.

———— ■ ————

The boys hovered around the tailgate of the pickup truck and watched as Grandpa filleted the fish he and the boys had caught at the pond. "Hey, boys, do you know what it means to be self-righteous?"

"It means that you think you're better than somebody else," Jeb said.

"Or that you know more than certain people," Bruce said.

"I think it means that you know you're right, and you want everybody else to know you're right," Spencer said.

"Those are all good answers," Grandpa said. "Let me tell you something Jesus said about this. He was teaching His followers how to pray, and He said, 'When you pray, do not be like the hypocrites! They love to stand up and pray in the houses of worship and on the street corners, so that everyone will see them. I assure you, they have already been paid in full. But when you pray, go to your room, close the door, and pray to your Father, who is unseen. And your Father, who sees what you do in private, will reward you." (See Matthew 6:5–6 TEV.)

As the boys walked back to the house and got cleaned up for dinner, they talked about things people do just to show off what they have or what they know—trying to call attention to the good deeds they do or trying to impress people with how spiritual they are.

Later that evening at the dinner table, Grandpa asked if anyone would like to pray.

"I'll pray," Bruce volunteered. And then he began, "Thank You, God, for this day and all the great fish we caught. Thank You that we aren't like those hypocrites …"

Even though it was in the middle of a prayer, all of the boys and Grandpa had to laugh.

Remember

"First take the log out of your own eye,
and then you will be able to see clearly to
take the speck out of your brother's eye."
Matthew 7:5 TEV

NOBODY LIKES A SHOW-OFF.

You Can Do It!

It takes skill to convince a person that you are right without that person deciding you are a know-it-all. Ask the Lord to help you learn the art of gentle persuasion.

A Hard Decision

The best discipline, maybe the only discipline that really works, is self-discipline.

———— ■ ————

Chance stared hard and long at the trays of cookies on the dining table. There must have been a hundred of them! He could tell from the sight and the aroma that they were his favorite—pecan, chocolate chip, and oatmeal cookies!

Chance looked around. There was no one in sight.

"Who would miss just one cookie from this whole table?" he said aloud to himself.

"Somebody might have counted them out for a special deal," he answered himself, suddenly remembering that Mom was in charge of a big party at school.

"But why did she have to make my favorite? She knew that would drive me crazy if I saw the cookies here on the table," he said to himself.

"She probably made your favorite because these are for you and your class tomorrow," he replied to himself.

"Nobody will ever know I was the one who took a cookie," he said to himself.

Just at that moment his sister Heather walked into the dining room. "Are you alone?" she asked. "I thought I heard voices arguing."

"Yeah, I'm alone," Chance said, a little embarrassed that his sister had caught him talking to himself.

"What were you arguing with yourself about?" Heather asked.

"Doesn't matter," Chance said as he started to walk out of the dining room.

"Who won the argument?" Heather teased.

"My better self," Chance said. "The me that really wants a cookie but doesn't want to get caught stealing one—and who is hoping that tomorrow I'll get one anyway. I've got to get out of here because the smell is driving me crazy! That's who."

Remember

The Spirit produces ... self-control.
Galatians 5:22–23 TEV

GOD WILL HELP YOU RESIST
TEMPTATION.

You Can Do It!

Do God's will, and ask Him to give you His power. That will give you real willpower.

Giving the Best

That man is a success . . . who looked for the best in others and gave the best he had.

——— ■ ———

Everybody who knew David knew he loved playing with toys. It really was no wonder he had more toys than just about any boy he knew. David had a great imagination, and it didn't take much for him to come up with a story and lots of action with just about any type of toy!

"What do you want for Christmas?" Mama had asked last night. "Toys!" David said. He began to list toys he wanted. To his surprise, Mama said, "Well, David, those sound like good ideas. But first you need to give away six toys you already have."

"Why?" David asked.

"Because," Mama said, "you need to make room for the new toys, and there are boys who don't have any toys. Think about which toys you'd like to give away."

David sorted through his room and finally came up with six toys he thought he could do without. They really were his oldest toys, and one of them was just a little broken. He took them out to his mother.

"David," she said, "you have a good imagination, so I want you to imagine what it would be like if you didn't have any toys." That was hard to do, but David thought he could imagine not having toys. "Now," Mama said, "if you didn't have any toys, are the toys in this box the ones you would like to receive?"

David hung his head. "No," he said. "Not really."

"Christmas is about giving, David—not getting. God gave us His Son Jesus and that was His very best gift to us. We need to give our best. Use your imagination to think up the best toys to give."

David had never thought about using his imagination when it came to giving...it sounded like playing to him. And that was easy!

Whatever you do, do well.
Ecclesiastes 9:10 NLT

HE WHO GIVES WILL RECEIVE.

What is it that you can give this year at the holiday season? Make your concerns for what you are giving as great as your concerns about what you'd like to receive.

INDEX

ACKNOWLEDGMENTS

Father Jerome Cummings (8), Charles R. Swindoll (10), Mark Twain (12, 184), Bill Cosby (14), John Mason (16), Jim Beggs (18), A. A. Milne (20, 290), D. Jackman (22), Gloria Copeland (24), John Chrysostom (26), Andrew Murray (28), John Dryden (30), Aeschylus (32), Henry Ford (34, 84), Leonard Ravenhill (36), Henry Ward Beecher (38), John Stamos (40), Henry David Thoreau (42), Anonymous (44, 56, 60, 64, 90, 94 128, 130, 136, 140, 148, 174, 176, 178, 180, 188, 192, 206, 220, 226, 228, 232, 238, 242, 268, 292, 304, 306), Izaak Walton (46), Thomas Merton (48), Ralph Waldo Emerson (50, 260), David Starr Jordan (52), Mother Teresa (54), William Hazlitt (58), Edith Wharton (62), St. Francis of Assisi (66), R. C. Sproul (68), Sir Wilfred Grenfell (70), Alan Stewart Paton (72), Mary Gardiner Brainard (74), Sir Edmund Hillary (76), Woodrow Wilson (78), George Washington (80), St. Basil (82), Abraham Lincoln (86), John Wesley (88), Arnold Lobel (92), Italian Proverb (96), English Proverb (98), Traditional Proverb (100), John Wayne (102), John Hockenberry (104), Henry Wadsworth Longfellow (106), David Joseph Swartz (108), George A. Buttrick (110), John Burroughs (112), William Shakespeare (114), Elbert Hubbard (116), Scottish Proverb (118), Ken Blanchard (120), G. K. Chesterton (122), Cecil Frances Alexander (124), Miguel de Cervantes (126), Nicholas Boileau-Despreaux (132, 134), Maya Angelou (138), Laura Ingalls Wilder (142), French Proverb (144), Jean Kirkpatrick (146), Johanna Spyri (150), Carlo Collodi (152), Frankie Byrne (154), Dutch Proverb (156, 274), Horace Bushnell (158), Alex Haley (160), William Penn (162), Wilbur Wright (164), Pearl Bailey (166), David O. McKay (168), Dave

REFERENCES